PHILLIP DEAN was born in rural Queensland and is a graduate of the Queensland College of Art and the University of Queensland. His writing for theatre includes *Long Gone Lonesome Cowgirls*, *First Asylum*, and adaptations of the Nick Earls' novels *After January* and *Zigzag Street* for La Boite, *Seeking True South* (libretto) for Opera Qld, and *Bob Cat Dancing* for Queensland Biennial Festival of Music. Philip is the winner of a Matilda Award and an AWGIE Award. He lives in Brisbane.

NICK EARLS Nick is the author of fifteen books, including the bestselling novels *Zigzag Street* (winner of a Betty Trask Award in the UK in 1998), *Perfect Skin* and *After January*. *48 Shades of Brown* was awarded Book of the Year (Older Readers) by the Children's Book Council of Australia in 2000, and was a Kirkus Reviews book of the year selection in the US in 2004. Five of his novels have been adapted into stage plays and two into feature films.

48 SHADES OF BROWN

Adapted by Philip Dean

from the novel by Nick Earls

Currency Press • Sydney

CURRENCY PLAYS

First published in 2001
by Currency Press Pty Ltd,
PO Box 2287, Strawberry Hills, NSW, 2012, Australia
enquiries@currency.com.au
www.currency.com.au

in association with La Boite Theatre, Brisbane Copyright © Phillip Dean,
2001; Sandra Gattenhof and La Boite Theatre, Teachers' Notes, 2001.

Reprinted 2003, 2006, 2010, 2012 (twice), 2013, 2015, 2016, 2017, 2019, 2020.

NATIONAL LIBRARY OF AUSTRALIA CIP DATA

Author: Dean, Phillip, 1954–.
Title: 48 shades of brown / Phillip Dean.
ISBN: 9780868196527 (pbk.)
Other Authors/Contributors:
                Earls, Nick, 1963–. La Boite Theatre (Brisbane, Qld.)
Dewey Number: A822.3

Publication of this title was assisted by the Commonwealth
Government through the Australia Council, its arts funding
and advisory body.

Australian Government

Contents

48 SHADES OF BROWN

ACT ONE   1

ACT TWO   30

Teachers' Notes   59

Typeset by Emily Ralph for Currency Press.
Cover design by Sasha Middleton, Toadshow.
Cover image: Tony Brockman, Rebecca Murphy, Michael Dorman and Cara McIlveen from La Boite Theatre's 2001 production (Photo: Rob MacColl).
Currency Press acknowledges the Traditional Owners of the Country on which we live and work. We pay our respects to all Aboriginal and Torres Strait Islander Elders, past and present.

For Miette

48 Shades of Brown was first produced by La Boite Theatre, Brisbane, on 3 May 2001, with the following cast:

DAN	Michael Dorman
JACQ	Rebecca Murphy
NAOMI/IMOGEN/ CLARE/GIRL/INGA	Cara McIlveen
CHRIS/JASON/PHIL	Tony Brockman

Director, Jean-Marc Russ
Designer, Geoff Corbett
Lighting Designer, George Meijer
Sound Designer, Campbell Misfeld
Stage Manager, Sonya Leigh Bohlen
Assistant to the Director, Kristy Mayer

Characters

DAN, aged sixteen

JACQ, Dan's Aunt, aged twenty-three

NAOMI, aged eighteen

CHRIS, Dan's mate, aged sixteen

IMOGEN, aged sixteen

CLARE, an actor in her teens

GIRL, aged about sixteen

INGA, a Danish girl about sixteen

JASON, aged twenty-one

PHIL, aged about thirty

The parts of CLARE, GIRL and INGA should be played by the actor playing IMOGEN.

The parts of JASON and PHIL should be played by the actor playing CHRIS.

ACT ONE

We can see a bedroom and the back veranda of a share house in Toowong. The room has a bed, a chair and desk, and a waste paper bin. There are chairs on the veranda and perhaps a table and steps down to the back yard. There is a telephone near the entrance to the rest of the house.

At the moment though, we are in the carpark at Brisbane airport. DAN *is 16.* JACQ *is a 23-year-old uni student. She has short hair and is fashionable with a techno flavour.*

JACQ: So how was Geneva? Dan?

DAN: Sorry.

JACQ: Oh, right.

DAN: Just give me a minute.

> *Pause.*

JACQ: Can I… Is there anything I can do?

DAN:No.

> *Pause.*

JACQ: Anything your mother would do?

DAN: She'd probably leave me alone.

JACQ: Sorry.

> DAN *breathes carefully, recovering slightly.*

DAN: You're not patting me. That's good.

JACQ: Patting?

DAN: I'm sure you've patted a vomiting person before.

JACQ: I think I'd be more conscious of holding their hair out of the way.

DAN: Holding their hair?

JACQ: Yeah, you know, long hair.

DAN: Right.

JACQ: Feeling better?

DAN: I think I'm all right.

> DAN *is about to pick up the luggage.*

JACQ: There's no hurry.

DAN: Thanks.

JACQ: I was thinking of the car.

DAN: Right.

JACQ: So, how was Geneva?

DAN: Cold and grey, mostly. I don't know if there is a time of year when Geneva buzzes, but I hope it's not January.

JACQ: Your parents are in for an excellent year, then.

DAN: Yeah. And lots of snow. That's why I'm late.

JACQ: I told school. It's not a problem. There was a guy in your class… Chris?

DAN: Chris Burns.

JACQ: He was going to, you know, do whatever. Get books, or whatever.

DAN: Good. Thanks.

> *Pause.*

I'm fine now.

JACQ: I'll go and get the car. Save you walking.

> JACQ *leaves.*

DAN: That'd be quite personal, wouldn't it, Dan? Holding a girl's hair out of her vomit trajectory. She'd have to be quite interested before she'd let you do that. [*He picks up his bag.*] Okay. Do not throw up in the car, Dan. That is not how you want to begin this year.

> *Meanwhile* NAOMI *has come onto the house veranda and is making a mess of the Sunday paper. She is blond, pretty and eighteen.* DAN *stares at her for a moment before picking up his suitcase and moving towards her.* JACQ *enters.*

JACQ: Any calls?

NAOMI: No. Did the plane arrive?

JACQ: Eventually. I should have been at band practice half an hour ago.

NAOMI: Hi Dan.

JACQ: This is Naomi. She always gets the paper last. It's a rule.

> NAOMI *looks innocent.*

DAN: Hi.

NAOMI: So how was Geneva?

JACQ: Not the vomit question.

DAN: I did not vomit.

JACQ: I was ready to pat him, you know.

NAOMI: Will we have to pat him a lot this year?

JACQ: Only when he's sick. He likes to be patted when he is sick.

NAOMI: Sure. It's comforting.

> DAN *is growing increasingly annoyed.*

DAN: Could we stop this?

JACQ: Madge isn't here and someone's got to look after you.

DAN: Jacq.

JACQ: I'm sure you can look after yourself.

DAN: Thank you.

JACQ: And it's going to be a great year.

NAOMI: Absolutely.

JACQ: I'm late. Now you kids be nice to each other.

> JACQ *leaves. Pause.*

NAOMI: Band practice.

DAN: Are they any good?

NAOMI: I don't know.

> NAOMI *shuffles the pages of the paper and folds them into a wad. She seems pleased. She stands and stretches. She wears a white cheese cloth dress that is somewhat see-through.* DAN *is mesmerized.*

NAOMI: Your father works for a bank?

DAN: A bank… oh, yeah. Yeah.

NAOMI: And your mother?

DAN: No. She doesn't.

NAOMI: Right.

DAN: My mother… is going to work on her French.

NAOMI: And what will she do with her French, when she's worked on it?

DAN: Speak to French people, I suppose.

NAOMI: Do you speak French?

DAN: No.

NAOMI: Neither do I.

DAN: What do you do?

NAOMI: I'd use a phrase book, I suppose.

DAN: And what do you do at uni?

NAOMI: Oh. Sorry. Psychology. Second year. Well, when the semester starts it'll be second year. And I work in a deli. Not far from here.

Pause.

DAN: What made you pick psychology?

NAOMI: I don't know. I just did.

DAN: Right.

Pause.

I should unpack things.

NAOMI *helps him with his things. They move towards his room.*

NAOMI: You must be tired. How long was the flight?

DAN: About 22 hours.

NAOMI: God. This is a good room. I was nearly going to swap.

DAN: I hope I don't disappoint it.

NAOMI: It's been kind of strange having all your stuff here for months and not having met you.

DAN: Jacq said you'd gone home for Christmas. Where's that?

NAOMI: We've got a sheep station out west. Do you need a hand?

DAN: No, no. I'm fine. Thanks Naomi.

NAOMI *smiles and pats* DAN *on the back.*

NAOMI: That's all right, Dan.

NAOMI *leaves.* DAN *throws his bag down.*

DAN: That went well, Dan. They both think you're a twelve year old.

DAN *opens his case and sits on the bed. He flops back exhausted. A late afternoon sun creeps over the house. Voices through the thin wall wake him up. He begins unpacking. In the next room* NAOMI *giggles. We hear the creaking of bed springs, followed by the rhythmic banging of the bed head against the wall.* DAN *nods along to the beat, then realizes what he's listening to.*

Oh, my God. [*He puts his hands over his ears, but takes them away after a moment.*] Be cool, Dan. [*He is anything but cool.*] You could've warned me. I mean is there an etiquette to this? Being in a room next to a housemate having sex? There is so much you don't know, Dan.

He continues unpacking until NAOMI *appears in a T-shirt, a bare-chested* JASON *behind her.* DAN *doesn't know where to look.*

NAOMI: Dan, you awake?

DAN: Yeah.

NAOMI: Want a beer?

JASON *puts an arm around* NAOMI *and waves a bottle in* DAN*'s direction.*

DAN: Ah… no. Thanks. I'm a bit jetlagged.

NAOMI *and* JASON *take their beers to the veranda.*

NAOMI: We're back at uni in two weeks.

JASON: Yeah.

NAOMI: I still haven't decided what subjects I'm doing.

JASON: Right.

NAOMI: That party next Saturday?

JACQ: Yeah.

NAOMI: Are we still going?

JASON: S'pose.

DAN *joins them.*

DAN: I finished unpacking.

NAOMI: Dan, this is Jason.

DAN: Hi.

JASON: So you've just moved in, yeah?

DAN: Today.

JASON: You in first-year?

NAOMI: No, this is Jacq's… ah…

DAN: Nephew.

NAOMI: That means she's your aunt. Weird.

DAN: My mother's 21 years older than Jacq.

NAOMI: Are they alike? I haven't met your mother.

DAN: You have, I think. When she was moving my stuff in.

NAOMI: That was your mother?

JASON: So who else would it have been? Did you just think he liked older women, or something?

NAOMI: We passed on the steps. I didn't think about it.

JASON: [*finishing his beer*] Well, I gotta go.

NAOMI: Now?

JASON: I'm bored.

NAOMI: I'll ring you tomorrow.

JASON: If you want.

> JASON *leaves.*

DAN: He seems nice.

NAOMI: Feel better after a sleep?

DAN: Yeah.

JACQ: [*entering*] Hi kids. [*To* NAOMI] I think I just passed the best 15 seconds of your weekend on the way in.

NAOMI: Thanks Jacq.

JACQ: So he didn't hang around then?

NAOMI: He knew you were coming home. [*To* DAN] She doesn't like Jason very much.

> NAOMI *puts her arm around* JACQ.

Poor Jacq, you must have met some shitty men.

JACQ: The shittiest. And life is so uncomplicated without them. Just me and the thesis.

> *Phone rings.* NAOMI *crosses to answer it.*

Is there anything you need to do before tomorrow?

DAN: I don't think so.

NAOMI: Hello… Yeah, just a sec.

JACQ: Any getting ready for school stuff?

DAN: No.

NAOMI: Dan, it's for you. It's your mother.

> DAN *goes to the phone.*

DAN: Hello… You didn't say I should call… I just got here… A bit. I'll be all right after a night's sleep… If my plane had crashed you would have seen it on CNN hours ago… Okay… I'll send you an animal post card… Once a week like we agreed. Everything's fine… Bye. [*He hangs up.*] I didn't think we were doing phone calls. She gave me a stack of pre-paid post cards, but I didn't think we were doing phone calls.

DAN *leaves.*

NAOMI: How was band practice?

JACQ: You know. Lots of arguments, not much practice. I did come up with a name, though.

NAOMI: What?

JACQ: Crimplene.

NAOMI: That's good. Sounds a bit familiar.

JACQ: That's what I thought. But the others all said no.

NAOMI: It's the right kind of name. Yeah, I like it.

JACQ: You've got taste.

NAOMI: Thanks.

JACQ: In everything but men.

NAOMI: Jason's all right.

JACQ: Jason's not even partially right.

NAOMI: You just don't like him.

JACQ: There are so many better people out there.

NAOMI: I don't meet them.

JACQ: Ah, Naomi, don't be an idiot.

NAOMI: Thanks.

JACQ: I didn't mean it like that.

NAOMI: I'm going to make dinner.

> NAOMI *leaves.*

JACQ: Naomi!

> JACQ *follows her.* CHRIS *enters in his school uniform and carrying a bag. He looks around.*

CHRIS: Oi, Banger!

> DAN *enters, also in uniform and with school bag.*

DAN: Chris.

CHRIS: How was the trip?

DAN: Good. Cold.

CHRIS: Who's this Jack guy? I got a message through the office that Jack had called and I had to sort out your books and timetable and stuff. I thought you were staying with your aunt.

DAN: Yeah, that's Jacq.

> CHRIS *gives him a dubious look.*

Her name's Jacqueline. But no one calls her that.

CHRIS: Jacq. Doesn't sound right for your mother's sister.

DAN: She's not like my mother. She's 23, she's at uni, she plays bass in a band.

CHRIS: And you're staying with this person?

DAN: I'm sharing a house with her, yeah. And another uni student, Naomi.

CHRIS: How old's she?

DAN: 18.

CHRIS: This is sounding good. What's she like?

DAN: She's nice. You'd like Naomi. They're both pretty cool.

CHRIS: Yeah?

DAN: What happened at your place yesterday? Washing? Lawn mowing?

CHRIS: And a barbecue in the afternoon. The cousins came over.

DAN: At my place no one barbecued anything. They drank beer most of the afternoon and Naomi and her boyfriend had sex while I was unpacking my socks.

CHRIS: In your room? With you right there?

> *Pause.*

DAN: No, in the next room. But the walls are very thin.

CHRIS: I can't believe the year you're going to have.

DAN: And she came to my door afterwards and offered me a beer.

CHRIS: Straight afterwards? Like, still sweaty?

DAN: Still sweaty.

CHRIS: Joint projects, Dan. I think you and I should work together a lot this year.

DAN: Did you sort out my timetable?

> CHRIS *gets a pile of books from his bag.*

CHRIS: Yeah. And the year looks bad.

DAN: They always make it look bad at the beginning.

CHRIS: No, I've factored that in, and it still looks bad. This Naomi, what's she look like?

> DAN *has opened* Geometry *and* Calculus Three.

DAN: 'The indefinite integral notation for primitives.'

CHRIS: I told you.

DAN: I think I'll start working hard earlier this year. Instead of leaving it to the end.

CHRIS: Absolutely. Have you seen her naked?

DAN: What?

CHRIS: Accidentally opened the door when she's in the shower, that sort of thing?

JACQ: [*entering*] Hey Dan!

> JACQ *goes into* DAN*'s room, picks up the book,* Miss Smilla's Feeling for Snow. DAN *moves towards his room carrying the calculus book.* CHRIS *continues as though* DAN *is still beside him.*

CHRIS: Or, or, you'll like this, wake her up in the morning with a coffee, she might sleep naked.

> *Lights fade on* CHRIS.

JACQ: I've been going to read this. Any good?

DAN: I haven't read it yet. I have learned to say the title in the original Danish, though. '*Froken Smilla's fornemelse for sne.*'

JACQ: Well you never know when that might come in useful.

DAN: That's what I thought. One day I run into a Danish girl, she's lonely and homesick – but in an endearing way, she's devastatingly attractive and speaks only a bit of English. No, no, I'll say, your English is very good. The only Danish I know is, *Froken Smilla's fornemelse for sne*. Which will greatly impress her.

JACQ: And despite the language barrier she'll jump straight into bed with you.

DAN: Possibly.

JACQ: How's the study?

DAN: You know…

NAOMI: [*entering*] Hi, guys.

JACQ: Hi.

DAN: … difficult. Hi.

JACQ: Can I help?

DAN: Only if you know something about calculus.

NAOMI: [*joining them*] Calculus?

DAN: Yeah.

NAOMI: He's the guy with the little glasses and the long coat. The professor.

DAN: Thanks.

NAOMI: That's okay. If there's anything else, you know where I am. [*She frowns in thought for a moment.*] A green coat I think.

> NAOMI *smiles and leaves.*

JACQ: That was Naomi. She's from another planet.

DAN: Professor Calculus, from *Tin Tin.*

JACQ: I thought you meant maths.

DAN: I should have been specific.

JACQ: Can you cook anything?

DAN: Well, there's this thing I do where I put a lot of vegemite on a sandwich, cover the outside with butter and fry it.

JACQ: Very funny.

DAN: You mean what can I cook?

JACQ: Yeah.

DAN: Oh… the usual.

JACQ: Well, whenever you cook the usual, you can leave the washing up to the rest of us.

DAN: Okay. Oh, right.

JACQ: You have done washing up before?

DAN: Yeah. Of course.

JACQ: No hurry.

> JACQ *hands* DAN *the book and leaves.*

DAN: *Froken Smilla's fornemelse for sne.*

INGA: Ohhhh.

> DAN *turns as the lights change. He finds* INGA *on his bed.*

DAN: Hi. You must be Inga from Denmark.

INGA: Ya.

> DAN *joins her on the bed.*

DAN: And you don't speak any English.

INGA: Ya.

DAN: But luckily I know some Danish. *Froken Smilla's fornemelse for sne.*

INGA: Ohhhh.

JACQ: (*off*) Dan!

DAN: I can't have sex with you though. I've got to do the washing up.

> DAN *climbs off the bed, Inga leaves, the lights return to normal.* DAN *looks wistfully at the book for a moment before throwing it onto his desk. He joins* CHRIS *at school.*

CHRIS: Banger.

DAN: Friction.

CHRIS: Watch *The Simpsons* last night?

DAN: No, we were doing the grocery shopping.

CHRIS: Grocery shopping?

DAN: For food. You know that stuff you eat.

CHRIS: I thought it just appeared in the fridge.

DAN: No, no, you have to buy it.

CHRIS: Amazing. And then?

DAN: Beer and pizza in front of the TV. And for once this week, no one had sex.

CHRIS: Monday, no one had sex on Monday.

DAN: [*looking at* CHRIS] I think you're a bit over-involved.

CHRIS: So it's going well?

DAN: You know how to use a washing machine?

CHRIS: Don't be stupid.

DAN: I'll feel like an idiot if I have to ask Jacq or Naomi.

CHRIS: There must be instructions.

DAN: No, I looked.

CHRIS: You're on your own here, mate.

DAN: Thanks.

CHRIS: No problem. I might drop over on Saturday.

DAN: This Saturday?

CHRIS: Yeah.

DAN: It's my first weekend in the house. Can we leave for another weekend?

> *The bell rings.*

CHRIS: Yeah, all right. *Next* weekend. Let's go to Biology

DAN: I haven't got the text book yet.

CHRIS: [*opening the book and passing it to* DAN] Then you've missed out on page 247.

DAN: Don't you get enough porn on the Internet?

CHRIS: Yeah, but read the caption.

DAN: 'Sexual intercourse – left leg of female omitted.'

CHRIS: What are they trying to teach us, Dan?

DAN: Come on, we'll be late.

CHRIS: I mean how many one-legged girls do you know?

> *They move off as* JACQ *and* NAOMI *enter, both dressed to go out.*

NAOMI: What's the time now?

JACQ: Ten past nine.

NAOMI: [*picking up the phone, dialing*] I did say eight-thirty, didn't I?

JACQ: Eight-thirty and don't be late, as I recall.

NAOMI: It probably just means he got delayed, or something.

JACQ: It probably just means he's a thoughtless shithead. I say we give him another five seconds and go without him.

NAOMI: [*putting down the phone*] No answer, so he's probably on his way.

JACQ: Or gone off somewhere else and forgotten. No, not forgotten, he does this on purpose.

NAOMI: I'm sorry.

JACQ: Hey, don't apologize for him.

NAOMI: Can we give him another five minutes?

JACQ: Yeah, sure. I don't mind for myself, you know. It's just the attitude.

NAOMI: Treat 'em mean, keep 'em keen.

JACQ: [*shuddering in disgust*] Awww.

> DAN *enters.*

NAOMI: Still studying?

DAN: Yeah.

JACQ: You don't mind staying home on your own?

DAN: Of course not. I don't expect you to stay home all year.

JACQ: I mean you'd be entirely welcome, but…

DAN: I know. I'll do a bit more study, sort out my washing for the morning.

JACQ: Do it early if you're going to, the landlord's coming to fix the laundry tap. And he usually takes a while.

NAOMI: Because he likes visiting.

JACQ: You haven't met Phil the film-maker, have you? With his jungle outfit.

DAN: What's he film?

JACQ: Possums in the back yard, mainly, but he likes to look the part.

JASON enters.

NAOMI: Jason.

JASON: So are you ready then?

JACQ: Actually, we've been ready since eight-thirty.

NAOMI: Come on.

NAOMI leaves.

JASON: Are you coming, Dan?

DAN: No.

JASON: Should be a good night. Bit of dancing, lot of drinking, plenty of babes.

JACQ: Naomi's waiting for us.

JASON: Oh that's right, children aren't allowed into clubs are they?

JACQ: Jason, get in the car. [*She pushes him off. To* DAN] He's a bastard, ignore him.

DAN: It's okay.

JACQ: I'd better go.

JASON, NAOMI and JACQ leave. DAN is furious.

DAN: Right! Fine! And thanks, Mum. Thanks for dumping me here and leaving me to deal with all this when I've got my final year of school to worry about. It's not fair. I am never going to fit in here!

The lights change. A GIRL appears on the veranda, he moves towards her.

GIRL: What would it take?

DAN: What?

GIRL: To feel at home here?

DAN: I don't know. I've never felt more useless than I have this week, and I'm at least as useful as I've ever been. I'm not part of this.

GIRL: But if you had a girlfriend, like me, who dropped over, sometimes even when you weren't expecting her, who just liked hanging out here...

DAN: Yeah, sometimes being smart and sometimes being funny...

GIRL: And sometimes whisking you off to a two minute bouncy place.
DAN: Then I'd feel right at home.

He walks away and the GIRL *disappears.*

But it's not going to happen, Dan. So stop thinking about it.

A bright morning sun. JACQ *comes out.*

JACQ: Have you got the rent?
DAN: Yeah, I do.
JACQ: Doing your washing?
DAN: Yeah.

DAN *gives her the money.*

JACQ: Lovely.

Pause.

DAN: Um, we've got a computerized one at home, washing machine.
JACQ: A computerized washing machine?
DAN: Fisher and Paykel.
JACQ: Really?
DAN: So, I, ah, I'm not sure how this one works.
JACQ: Because ours is so different from the one you're used to?
DAN: Yeah.
JACQ: You've never done laundry before, have you?
DAN: I have.

Pause.

I've hung it out. Once or twice.
JACQ: Not big on chores, are we?
DAN: I'm beginning to realize this.
JACQ: And the washing up…
DAN: I've been doing the washing up.
JACQ: You have. But a bit less detergent and a bit more rinsing would be good. Whenever I pour a glass of water it has froth on it.
DAN: Yeah, all right.
JACQ: Fill the machine about three quarters with warm water. One scoop of washing powder, put in the clothes and turn the knob to wash. I'll explain rinsing and spinning when you get there.
DAN: Thanks.

NAOMI *enters from the shower.*

JACQ: Have you got the rent?

DAN *leaves.*

NAOMI: I'll get it. He didn't ring while I was in the shower, did he?

JACQ: No he didn't.

NAOMI: I thought you were going to band practice.

JACQ: I will be a bit later.

NAOMI: How's it going? Will I be buying your CD's soon?

JACQ: There are some bits of bass playing I haven't quite cracked yet. The attitude I can do. The black T-shirt I can do. The cigarette between the strings I can do. It's the bit with the fingers I'm no good at.

NAOMI: I would've thought that was one of the main bits.

JACQ: You would've been right. But I'll get there. We've got to knock Bananarama out of the *Guinness Book of Records* as the best selling girl band. That's a disgrace.

NAOMI: Not the Spice Girls?

JACQ: Let me believe that a girl band that plays their own instruments has a chance.

DAN *enters, picks up a basketball.*

NAOMI: Whatcha up to, Dan?

DAN: Washing.

NAOMI *knocks the ball out of his hand and dribbles it.* DAN *tries to steal it back.*

JACQ: Outside, children.

NAOMI *takes the ball into the yard where they continue to dribble and steal it from each other.* JACQ *sits on the steps watching.*

NAOMI: You're not bad.

DAN: You're pretty good yourself.

NAOMI: Played netball at school.

DAN: Netball's for girls.

NAOMI: Oh yeah?

She steals the ball with a flourish.

JACQ: Way to go Naomi!

The phone rings. JACQ *goes to answer it.* NAOMI *stops playing, still holding the ball.*

DAN: We need a hoop. If we had a hoop then we'd see who knew their stuff. Not that you're not good. I'm impressed.

JACQ: [*simultaneously on phone*] Hello… Oh, hi… Yeah… Okay, see you then.

JACQ *returns to the steps.* NAOMI *looks at her enquiringly.*

Just Lisa about band practice.

NAOMI *throws the ball to* DAN *and goes to sulk on the veranda.*

DAN: [*quietly to* JACQ] Did I do something?

JACQ: No.

DAN: I was joking about the netball.

JACQ: You know what sort of mood Jason was in last night. Eventually they had a big argument he went off with some mates.

DAN: So, is it over between them?

JACQ: Not for Naomi.

DAN: She could do so much better.

JACQ: You'll get no argument from me.

DAN: She deserves someone nice.

JACQ: Anyone in mind?

DAN: I'm just saying.

PHIL: [*offstage*] Anyone home?

DAN *turns towards the voice.* JACQ *and* NAOMI *escape inside.* PHIL *enters.*

PHIL: Daniel is it?

DAN: Yeah.

PHIL: I'm Phil, your landlord.

DAN: Hi.

PHIL: The girls here?

DAN: Yeah they're… [*turning to find them gone*]… probably still asleep. They went out last night.

PHIL: Ah, right. I inherited this place, you know. And I've been lucky, always had good tenants, but none better than Jacqueline. [*He looks about.*] Some of those trees could do with a bit of pruning. I could come back next weekend and do that. What do you think?

DAN: Yeah, sure.

PHIL: You like films?

DAN: I suppose.

PHIL: Dugong habitats. That's my thing at the moment. I spend most of my time up to my armpits in dugong habitats. There's a lot of people that don't know much about the dugong.

DAN: I can imagine.

PHIL: Anyway, let's have a look at this tap, and I'll tell you all about it.

> PHIL *leaves.* JACQ *approaches.* NAOMI *returns to the veranda.*

JACQ: You got the whole run-down on the dugong doco?

DAN: Pretty much shot for shot.

JACQ: I should've warned you. We can't keep him away from the place. But he did fix the tap?

DAN: Yeah.

JACQ: And he didn't find anything to invite himself back to do, did he?

DAN: No. No, apart from a bit of tree pruning.

JACQ: So that's a yes, then.

DAN: Next Sunday, same time.

JACQ: What is it with him? What's the attraction? I mean you'd think he'd be away a lot, filming things, but no.

DAN: I'm a lot better informed about dugongs now.

JACQ: And you never know when that might be useful.

> DAN *goes inside.*

JACQ: What time do you have to be at work?

NAOMI: One o'clock.

JACQ: I can give you a lift on the way to band practice.

NAOMI: Thanks, that'd be good.

> *Pause.*

He rang before.

JACQ: I wondered if it was him.

NAOMI: He said he was sorry.

JACQ: Yeah, right. So does that mean you're going to that party tonight?

NAOMI: No. He has to do something for his father.

JACQ: We should have a party.

NAOMI: Tonight?

JACQ: No. When uni starts.

NAOMI: Yeah.

JACQ: Not next weekend, the one after.

> DAN *comes out with two coffees.*

NAOMI: You could play. Your band.

JACQ: You think?

NAOMI: It'd be great.

JACQ: We're talking about having a party.

DAN: Yeah, that'd be good.

JACQ: I'll ask them. I'm not sure that we'll be ready though. We only half know two songs.

DAN: I made you a coffee.

NAOMI: Dan, you are such a sweetie.

JACQ: We should go soon.

> JACQ *and* NAOMI *leave.* DAN *sits smiling for a moment then opens a book. It is now morning a week later.* CHRIS *comes into the yard.*

CHRIS: Banger.

DAN: Chris?

CHRIS: I told you I was coming over today. It's a bit early, I know. So where are these girls?

DAN: In bed, I guess.

CHRIS: Yeah, in bed?

DAN: Asleep.

CHRIS: Right. So what are you doing?

DAN: The English assignment.

CHRIS: The text thing?

DAN: Yeah. I'm doing *Romeo + Juliet*, the fish-tank scene.

CHRIS: There's a fish-tank in *Romeo and Juliet*?

DAN: In Baz Luhrmann's version.

CHRIS: But not in Shakespeare's.

DAN: I think he was pretty open about it really.

CHRIS: So the film's good?

DAN: Yeah, it is. Excellent. You should watch it.

CHRIS: I saw a bit. In class. Clare Danes is a babe.

DAN: I can't disagree with you there. Clare Danes is definitely a babe.

CHRIS: So tell me about these girls you live with. What about Naomi?

DAN: What about her?

CHRIS: You know.

DAN: We share the house. And she's got a boyfriend.

CHRIS: And if she didn't have a boyfriend?

DAN: Nothing would happen.

CHRIS: But you've thought about it?

DAN: No, I haven't thought about it. She's 18, I'm 16.

CHRIS: What if she made the first move?

DAN: It's not going to happen. So give me a break. I've just moved in. Uni'll start soon, they'll have friends dropping over. I'm taking a longer-term view here. I've got all year.

CHRIS: Longer-term view. I like that.

DAN: So just be cool, okay? And don't embarrass me.

CHRIS: You seem a bit tense, Dan.

> JACQ *come onto the veranda.*

DAN: Jacq, this is Chris.

NAOMI: Hi Chris.

CHRIS: Hi.

JACQ: You're the one who was getting everything sorted out while Dan was stuck in Europe.

CHRIS: Yeah.

DAN: We're going to work on an assignment.

JACQ: What's the assignment?

DAN: Biology.

CHRIS: [*simultaneous with* DAN] English.

JACQ: [*laughs*] Right.

> NAOMI *comes out with a cup of coffee.*

You're up early.

NAOMI: I've got to start work at eight-thirty.

DAN: Naomi, this is Chris.

NAOMI: Hi Chris. You guys doing assignments?

CHRIS: Yeah.

NAOMI: Did you finish that Professor Calculus thing?

DAN: Yeah, no problem.

CHRIS: What Professor Calculus thing?

NAOMI: For English, wasn't it?

DAN: Yes.

CHRIS: I thought you were doing *Romeo + Juliet*.

DAN: That's another possibility.

CHRIS: Is *Tin Tin* on the list?

DAN: No, but we can look beyond it.

CHRIS: Yeah, I guess.

NAOMI: I better get ready. It's so hot. I'm going to be a big sweatball by the time I get to work. Will you be here when I get home?

JACQ: Yeah, I think. I don't know about band practice.

NAOMI: Did you ask about the party?

JACQ: We're not ready. But I did organize a DJ.

NAOMI: Oh, brilliant. Nice to meet you, Chris.

CHRIS: You too.

> NAOMI *leaves.* JACQ *follows her out.*

CHRIS: Sweatball. How do you live here?

DAN: Chris.

CHRIS: She is practically inviting you to think of her sweating. Imagine that. Imagine that woman sweating. My God, she's fine.

DAN: As if I hadn't noticed.

> CHRIS *has picked up the basketball and moved into the yard.* DAN *follows him, mainly to keep him quiet. They toss the ball around.*

CHRIS: I knew you'd have to crack. She's just a room away. Ready to help with your assignments. Any help you want to give me, Naomi, I am ready!

DAN: Shut up, will you, Jacq's still here.

CHRIS: If she wanted to explain Mickey Mouse I'd be happy. And she's almost sleeping next to you.

DAN: There is a wall in between.

CHRIS: And Jacq. I never thought I'd fancy someone's aunt but…

DAN: Chris, shut up.

> JACQ *returns.*

CHRIS: Banger, it's just not fair.

> *Pause.*

JACQ: Don't stop talking on my account.

CHRIS: We were just discussing our assignments.
JACQ: Yeah, right. I'm going down the shop, won't be long.

> JACQ *leaves.*

CHRIS: So what's this about a party?
DAN: Next weekend.
CHRIS: Am I coming?
DAN: That depends.
CHRIS: Come on, you live here, you can invite me.
DAN: Yeah, all right, but you've got to be cool, okay?
CHRIS: I've been cool, haven't I?
DAN: Just ease up on the Naomi thing.
CHRIS: 'I'll be a big sweatball.' How's that supposed to make you feel?
DAN: Nothing is happening. She's got a boyfriend.
CHRIS: You don't have a chance, do you?
DAN: Not a chance.
CHRIS: It's too hot for this. What we need is cold beer.
DAN: There's some in the fridge.
CHRIS: And it's okay?
DAN: I paid for a third of it.
CHRIS: I can't believe how cool your life is. You can just do whatever you want. There's no one to nag you at all.

> CHRIS *goes into the house.*

DAN: He's never coming back, is he, Dan? Absolutely not.

> *Night descends.*

Okay, okay. The fish-tank… the fish-tank brings their virtual selves closer through the magnification of the water, while keeping their actual selves apart.

> DAN *smiles to himself.* CLARE *walks onto the veranda. She wears the white dress and wings from the film.*

CLARE: Oh, Daniel, Daniel. Wherefore art thou, Daniel?

> DAN *turns and walks towards her.*

DAN: Most people call me Dan. Glad you could come.
CLARE: Thank you so much for inviting me. I get tired of all those Hollywood parties.

DAN: You didn't mind the long flight?

CLARE: Not at all.

DAN: Can I get you a VB, some corn chips?

CLARE: That's not why I came.

DAN: No?

CLARE: Dan, I was wondering. Do you... I'm going to feel like such an idiot asking this, but do you have a girlfriend at the moment?

DAN: Well, as it happens...

CHRIS: I'm so relieved.

DAN: I'll come up.

> *But by the time he gets there she's gone. He closes the books on the table. A bright sun finds* PHIL *in the yard holding a large pair of pruning shears and surveying his work.* DAN *joins him.*

PHIL: I might have got a bit too close to the detail.

DAN: Pretty close to the tree too.

PHIL: Give it a couple of weeks, it'll grow back.

DAN: I'm sure.

PHIL: Jacqueline home?

DAN: She's at band practice.

PHIL: What are they like? Pretty interesting?

DAN: Haven't heard them. They were going to play for our party next week but Jacq says they're not ready.

PHIL: You're having a party?

DAN: Probably. Might be having a party. I'm not sure. I think it's fairly low-key. Just a few friends over. One or two friends.

PHIL: But you'd all be inviting people?

DAN: I'm not sure.

PHIL: I think I'd be free that night.

DAN: Oh, right.

PHIL: What night did you say?

DAN: Saturday.

PHIL: Yeah, I think I'll be free.

DAN: Well, good.

PHIL: Eight o'clock? Something like that?

DAN: I guess.

PHIL: Good, I'll see you then.

PHIL *leaves.* JACQ *and* NAOMI *arrive with picnic things.*

JACQ: You did what?

DAN: I think I might have invited Phil to the party.

JACQ: No. You didn't.

DAN: I don't know how it happened.

NAOMI: Phil's all right. I think it's nice that Dan invited him.

JACQ: What about here?

NAOMI: Yeah, here's good. Who's got the food?

JACQ: [*holding it up*] I have. You know, I didn't think, we could have stopped at your deli, used your staff discount.

NAOMI: I wouldn't eat food from there. There's a rat in the kitchen.

JACQ: I had lunch there the other day!

NAOMI: Well you didn't ask me first.

JACQ: Is that something I should do? Ask if there's a rat in the kitchen?

NAOMI: Anyway, I liked that place we stopped. I should have bought one of the basil plants. Lets stop on the way back.

JACQ: Sure. Dan gave me this blanket.

DAN: Sorry. My mother picked it.

NAOMI: It's nice. It'd be good for picnics.

JACQ: Yeah, that's an idea.

NAOMI: Classes start tomorrow.

JACQ: And we've got the party on Saturday.

NAOMI: Yeah, that'll be good.

DAN: I thought I'd invite Chris.

JACQ: Chris?

NAOMI: We're all inviting people, aren't we. I've invited a few.

JACQ: Yeah, we are.

DAN: And maybe he could sleep on the floor in my room.

JACQ: It's your floor.

DAN: And, ah, his, his mother might call.

JACQ: His mother might call?

DAN: It's possible. You know, just to check things out.

JACQ: Like what?

DAN: I don't know what. That you exist, I suppose. My mother's sister, that bit of you.

JACQ: As opposed to the other bit that intends to drug Chris and sell him into slavery.

DAN: That's just the kind of thing she doesn't need to know.

JACQ: I'll tell her it's a sleepover, shall I? With chocolate milk and cookies?

DAN: Whatever.

NAOMI: Did you notice that all the trees have their names on them? Don't you think that's impressive? There are people out there who can just go, oh that's a... whatever the scientific name is. Can remember all the names.

JACQ: They probably have to forget a lot of useful stuff to make room.

NAOMI: Well I think the kind of people who know things like that are very impressive. And every bit as useful as people who do Honours in Government.

JACQ: That wouldn't be hard.

DAN: The ducks look hungry.

> DAN *takes a piece of bread and moves off.*

JACQ: We'll be back here in a couple of days for classes. What's your timetable like?

NAOMI: Pretty good. Got Friday off.

JACQ: Way to go.

NAOMI: You remember last week I was supposed to be going to that party with Jason, and then he couldn't go?

JACQ: Yeah.

NAOMI: Apparently he did go.

JACQ: You're kidding.

NAOMI: I was the one invited to that party. I told him about it.

JACQ: I know.

NAOMI: And he's at the party with someone else. And he thinks there is nothing wrong with this.

JACQ: So you dumped him.

NAOMI: No. Do you think I should?

JACQ: Yes. Yes. Yes.

NAOMI: I don't know. Maybe I should give him a second chance.

JACQ: Don't even think about it.

NAOMI: You're probably right.

JACQ: Of course I'm right.

NAOMI: We're having coffee tomorrow, so maybe we can talk about it.

JACQ: Just keep the discussion simple. Something along the lines of, 'Jason, you're dumped. Goodbye.'

NAOMI: Dan's having fun.

JACQ: Come on.

> *They both leave.* DAN *comes on reading a book.* CHRIS *comes on.* *They are at school.*

CHRIS: Hey, Banger. Where you been?

> DAN *tucks the book under his arm.*

DAN: Library.

CHRIS: So have you got a plan yet?

DAN: Plan?

CHRIS: With Naomi.

DAN: I thought you were going to ease up on the Naomi thing.

CHRIS: Come on, Banger. You've got to at least have a plan. What if she dumps her boyfriend tomorrow and you don't have a plan?

DAN: Give it a rest will, you?

CHRIS: What are you studying? [*He grabs the book.*] *What Bird Is That?*

DAN: On the weekend we were down by the uni lakes and Naomi was very impressed that the scientific names were written on the trees. She said people who know that kind of stuff are very impressive.

CHRIS: And you thought learning tree names was a bit obvious, so you're doing birds.

DAN: Yes.

CHRIS: Ah-ha! I knew you'd have a plan.

DAN: It's more of a strategy, really.

CHRIS: Strategy's good. How does it work?

DAN: I'm not actually going to let her know that I've got an interest at any stage. I'm never going to mention school.

CHRIS: That's good.

DAN: And I'm going to make myself much more interesting.

CHRIS: How would you do that?

DAN: With the bird stuff.

CHRIS: And that's it?

DAN: Yeah. We can be sitting on the veranda or at the uni lakes and I can say, Isn't that a striated thornbill or *Acanthiza Lineata*?

CHRIS: And she'll say, Oh Dan, you've made me into a big sweatball?

DAN: She'll just be impressed.

CHRIS: And you're going to learn all these? There's a lot of birds.

DAN: Just a few basic species and colour types. I mean she's not going to know one duck from another, is she?

CHRIS: *Anas Gibberifrons*, you're going to memorise useless stuff like that?

DAN: What else has twelve years of school equipped me for, Chris, I'm playing to my strengths.

CHRIS: [*skeptical*] I don't know.

DAN: Just a few species and some different shades of brown.

CHRIS: Brown?

DAN: See your average bird, basically, is brown. But not to the expert. We know the difference between say, bright rufous and golden buff, or olive brown and rich chestnut. Or any of the possible 48 shades of brown that I've listed from this book.

CHRIS: Dan.

DAN: What?

CHRIS: Have you thought about getting her drunk?

DAN: This is much more subtle.

CHRIS: But will it work?

DAN: I don't know, Chris. I don't know.

> DAN *walks away.* CHRIS *goes off.* DAN *sits on the veranda studying.* NAOMI *comes out with two basil plants in pots.*

NAOMI: Hi Dan. Studying?

DAN: Yeah, trying too.

NAOMI: I won't disturb you.

DAN: It's fine.

> DAN *tries to concentrate on the book as* NAOMI *tends the plants, but he finds it difficult not to peer down the top of her shirt as she bends forward. Pleased with her work* NAOMI *sits back on her haunches and arches her back.*

NAOMI: So what do you think of them?

DAN: I'm sorry, I'm really sorry. I was… What?

NAOMI: They're good plants, aren't they?

DAN: Terrific. They look great. Very green.

NAOMI: What are you studying?

DAN: Calculus. Maths calculus. I have a problem about a wall, a hose and a ladder.

NAOMI: And that's got something to do with maths?

DAN: Apparently.

NAOMI: You never know when you might need that sort of information.

DAN: For example, if you had a very tall basil plant and you had to climb a ladder to water the top of it.

NAOMI: Basil's not about maths. If you can't have love in your life, you might as well have home-grown basil. That's what I say. [*To* JACQ *who has just entered*.] Does basil like the sun?

JACQ: Lots of sun, I think.

NAOMI: Good.

>NAOMI *goes inside to wash her hands.*

JACQ: She's formed a meaningful relationship with a basil plant.

DAN: Is that bad?

JACQ: It would be big step up from Jason.

DAN: It would.

>JACQ *turns to leave.*

JACQ: I'll leave you to your work. Banger.

>*Pause.*

That is your nickname isn't it?

DAN: No.

>*Jacq laughs.*

Well, maybe. But could we tell no one.

NAOMI: [*entering*] What's funny?

JACQ: Nothing. I thought you were going out?

NAOMI: No I'm… I'm…

>NAOMI *bursts into tears and leaves.* JACQ *follows.* DAN *does not know what to do. He takes his books into his room and continues to work. It is now night.* DAN *rips a page from his bank pad and crumples it.*

DAN: Right. A ladder, a hose and a girl. [*He looks again.*] Wall. That would be way too interesting. A ladder, a hose and a wall.

JACQ *comes in.*

JACQ: Talking to yourself, huh.

DAN: Maybe.

JACQ: Did you get some dinner?

DAN: Yeah.

JACQ *turns to leave.*

DAN: Are you going to tell me what's going on?

JACQ: Sorry. Yeah. [*She sits on the bed.*] Remember last weekend Naomi was going to go to a party but Jason said he couldn't go, so Naomi didn't go. But it turns out he went with someone else. Anyway, Naomi forgave him. Even though he seemed to think it was nothing.

DAN: She's too nice, Naomi.

JACQ: Way too nice. Because today he dumped her.

DAN: How could he do that? How could anyone dump Naomi?

JACQ: Because he's a complete bastard.

DAN: There are guys who aren't like him.

JACQ: Yeah?

DAN: I mean I wouldn't do what he did. You know, if I ever got in that position, going out with someone. I mean, what I'm saying is, there must be plenty of guys who behave reasonably.

JACQ: Guys like you?

DAN: Yeah, just like me.

Pause.

Is she okay?

JACQ: She'll get over it.

DAN: Should I pretend I don't know?

JACQ: She said it was okay to tell you.

DAN: Did she? She said that?

JACQ: Dan.

DAN: What?

JACQ: Don't be in such a hurry.

DAN: What do you mean? And I'm not in one. And if I wanted to be, why not?

JACQ: Be in a hurry then. But slightly less psychotic would be good.

JACQ leaves the room and slumps into a chair on the veranda. She lights a cigarette. DAN sits at his desk staring into space. Silence. We hear NAOMI enter the next room and the sounds of her undressing and getting into bed—the snap of elastic, the zip, the creak of the bed are strangely amplified. DAN sighs. He aims a ball of paper at the bin.

DAN: If it goes in Naomi wants me.

It misses.

Two out of three.

The light fades on DAN. JACQ is still on the veranda. She begins to cry.

END ACT ONE.

ACT TWO

DAN *and* NAOMI *are by the university lakes. Both with bags and food.*

DAN: No, it's good. I needed to look up some stuff for my essay.

NAOMI: How about we sit here…

DAN: The school library's pretty bad.

NAOMI: … under this… *Ficus Macrophylla.*

DAN: Sounds good.

NAOMI: A two-thousand-word assignment in week three, is that fair?

DAN: Not fair at all.

NAOMI: Uni'd be good without the assignments.

DAN: Should we throw some bread to the *Anas Gibberifrons*?

NAOMI: Trees don't eat bread, Dan.

DAN: I meant the ducks.

NAOMI: You know the names of ducks?

DAN: A few of them, I suppose.

NAOMI: Do they have a common name?

DAN: Yeah, that'd be the Grey Teal.

NAOMI: Really? Isn't that interesting?

DAN: Quite a common species.

NAOMI: No, I meant because they're not gray at all.

    DAN *peers in the direction of the ducks, momentarily defeated.*

DAN: That's one of the more interesting features of the Grey Teal.

NAOMI: That they're brown?

DAN: It's relative. Brown is such a bird colour that you'd be calling them all brown if you where honest. And that wouldn't be much use.

NAOMI: Yeah, lots of birds are brown, but not the same kind of brown.

DAN: Exactly. And the Grey Teal has grey-brown on its… ah… bits you can't see when it's in the water.

    Pause.

That one walking towards us must be a young one. The gray comes later.

NAOMI: It must be difficult keeping track of all those shades of brown. You'd have to have a name for each one.

DAN: Like bright rufous or tawny brown.

NAOMI: It'd be interesting to know how many there were.

DAN: 48.

NAOMI: Wow. How do you know this stuff?

DAN: Just something I picked up.

NAOMI: And these 48 browns are just for birds?

DAN: Yeah, otherwise you'd have to include words like caramel or beige, which aren't bird colours.

NAOMI: So what are they?

DAN: What?

NAOMI: The 48 shades of brown?

DAN: Well, I can't name them.

NAOMI: But you're sure there are 48?

DAN: Oh yeah, I've got them written down.

NAOMI: You've got them written down?

DAN: I think we should feed the ducks now.

NAOMI: Why would you do that?

DAN: They look very hungry.

NAOMI: We'd better feed them then.

They both leave. JACQ *enters.*

JACQ: Dan, you up!

She goes to his room. DAN *comes in without his shirt and with a piece of toast between his teeth. He finishes dressing for school as he talks.*

DAN: Ott?

JACQ: Just making sure you were up. I thought it was Naomi in the shower.

DAN: It is now.

JACQ: Oh shit.

DAN: Gotta be quick.

JACQ: I hear you had some bird stuff happening yesterday?

DAN: What did she say?

JACQ: That you're a bit of an expert on bird names.

DAN: Expert.

JACQ: You didn't learn them just for her benefit, did you?

DAN: I had to learn them for Biol.

JACQ: You're doing the human digestive system.

DAN: Stop paying such good attention. Okay, I learned a few bird names.

JACQ: Nothing obvious for you. You'd never turn up with a bunch of flowers and a box of chocolates.

DAN: We live in the same house.

JACQ: Beside the point.

DAN: That stuff is so…

JACQ: Obvious. Like I said. Like anxiety and acne it goes with the 16-year-old boys I remember.

DAN: Hey, I can do them. Easy. That's not the kind of guy I need to be. You seen my bag?

JACQ: It's on the veranda, and what's wrong with the kind of guy you are?

DAN: What I need is something that's ninety percent me and ten percent interesting.

JACQ: It sounds irresistible.

DAN: Well that's the plan.

JACQ: Where were the boys like you when I was 16?

DAN: Do you think I should water the basil?

JACQ: Well it's history unless someone looks after it. This basil thing with Naomi is all because of an ex who made great pesto. He went overseas. They never really broke up.

DAN: He's not coming back is he?

JACQ: Dan.

DAN: I know.

    CHRIS *enters. He's at school.* DAN *joins him.*

CHRIS: Were you in the library again?

DAN: Yeah.

CHRIS: You'll go blind.

DAN: I was on the Internet.

CHRIS: Like I said, you'll go blind.

    CHRIS *snatches some printed pages out of* DAN*'s hand.*

DAN: Chris.

CHRIS: This looks like a recipe.

DAN: It is.

CHRIS: 'Mike's two minute pesto.' Is there anything you want to tell me, Dan?

DAN: Food for the party.

CHRIS: Right, right, the party. Is that the sort of things they have at uni parties?

DAN: Absolutely.

CHRIS: So. Are you ready for this?

DAN: I think so.

CHRIS: It's going to be so cool. Uni girls. And I'm thinking they'll invite more girls than guys.

DAN: I don't know.

CHRIS: Imagine if I met a girl, with a car. What will it take? To score a uni girl?

DAN: That's the big question, isn't it?

CHRIS: So we've got to have a plan. We can't be there as ourselves.

DAN: Definitely not ourselves. I'm thinking worldly. We have to fake worldliness.

CHRIS: Exactly. We mention school once and we're dead. So we've got to be at uni too. And just about everyone there's going to be at Queensland uni, right?

DAN: Probably, yeah.

CHRIS: So QUT. We're at QUT.

DAN: But I've never been to QUT. I know what Queensland uni looks like. If we're faking it, I've got a better chance at Queensland uni. I can visualize it.

CHRIS: But you've never been a student there so you won't fool someone who has. No, QUT. Law at QUT.

DAN: Law.

CHRIS: Law is good. Everyone thinks Law is good.

DAN: But what do we know about it?

CHRIS: Nothing. But that's not what it's about. If you start thinking content's an issue, you're dead. This is about style. I mean if you were a law student and you started going on to some girl about what you'd been learning, do you think she'd be impressed? No. That's not what they're after.

DAN: I guess not.

Chris: And, and, and, it should be second-year law. Because if you were trying to fake it you'd say first-year, wouldn't you? So second-year law, QUT. That'll get them in.

DAN: I don't know that it will. I mean going on the uni women I know, they seem to like something more subtle. Like being able to make fresh pesto.

CHRIS: I don't think so.

DAN: I have it on good authority that there are uni women out there who are totally into basil-growing guys.

CHRIS: Way too weird. I think you're being too specific here. We've got to maximize our chances. Law QUT, that's what they'll go for. It's in the city and the parking sucks. That's all you need to know. Forget that other stuff.

DAN: And after? Once they're impressed with the QUT thing, where does the conversation go?

CHRIS: Them. They love talking about themselves. Play it cool. Make out like you're interested in them.

DAN: I am interested in them.

CHRIS: Law, QUT. We can't go wrong. Trust me, Dan.

> CHRIS *leaves.* NAOMI *approaches. They are in the backyard.*

NAOMI: Hey Dan, that bird, what is it?

DAN: I can't name them all, you know.

NAOMI: But I don't know anything about them. And it's brown, so I thought you'd know. Up there.

DAN: Ah, right. One of those.

NAOMI: What?

DAN: That, I'm pretty sure, is a Striated Thornbill.

NAOMI: Striated Thornbill.

DAN: Easily confused with the Brown Thornbill.

NAOMI: Fancy name?

DAN: *Acanthiza Lineata.*

NAOMI: Cool.

DAN: Definitely one of your cooler brown birds.

NAOMI: So tell me about it.

DAN: It migrates north for the winter. It eats mainly worms. It breeds in the spring, laying a maximum of six bluish eggs. It mates for life.

NAOMI: How sweet.

DAN: It has a batting average in the mid-thirties, never misses *The Simpsons*, and its favorite colour is brown.

NAOMI: I like this bird.

> *They both watch its flight.*

DAN: Maybe it's flying north early. To be truthful, I really don't know much about them.

NAOMI: I did wonder when you quoted its batting average.

> NAOMI *leaves.* DAN *goes to his room and removes his uniform.*

DAN: Dan, you are such a loser. The object of your most urgent desires thinks you're a bird-nerd. And you don't have a plan for the party.

> *The lights change.* JACQ, NAOMI *and* CHRIS *appear in his fantasy.* DAN *is standing in his boxer shorts.*

CHRIS: Are you ready for this?

NAOMI: We're all inviting people, aren't we?

JACQ: Don't be in such a hurry.

CHRIS: So what will it take? To get a uni girl? [*He approaches* NAOMI.] Hi, Chris. Second-year Law, QUT.

NAOMI: You look familiar.

CHRIS: You must've been dreaming about me.

> CHRIS *and* NAOMI *begin a passionate kiss.* DAN *runs to separate them.*

DAN: No! Naomi, what are you doing?

NAOMI: It's your fantasy, Dan.

DAN: It's my worse than worst-case scenario. I'm bracing myself for any possibility.

NAOMI: And how are you doing?

DAN: Not well. I'm quite unbraced.

NAOMI: What about that?

> DAN *turns to find* CHRIS *on his bed with* JACQ.

DAN: Ahh! No. Stop. Stop.

> *He runs to them but by the time he gets there* CHRIS *has disappeared.* NAOMI *leaves.* DAN *slumps in his chair. Reality is restored.*

JACQ: So are you ready for this party?

DAN: Oh, Jacq, sorry, what?

JACQ: Are you ready for this party? Are you getting dressed?

DAN: I think so. I don't know.

JACQ: You look a little tense.

DAN: Who did Naomi invite, do you know?

JACQ: I have no idea.

DAN: I just wondered.

JACQ: What's the problem?

DAN: I made some pesto.

JACQ: Sorry?

DAN: For the party. [*He picks up a bowl.*] I made some pesto.

JACQ: You made this yourself?

DAN: This morning.

JACQ: It looks good. You didn't decapitate Naomi's basil, did you?

DAN: No, I got it from the fruit shop.

JACQ: Ummm. Are the black bits pepper?

DAN: Pepper?

JACQ: Urgh.

DAN: What?

JACQ: Did you wash it, did you cut off the roots?

>DAN *grabs the bowl.*

It's terrific, other than that.

DAN: Other than the dirt.

JACQ: Relax, Dan. It's a party.

>DAN *throws the pesto into his waste paper bin and begins getting dressed.*

DAN: It never existed, right?

JACQ: Right.

NAOMI: [*entering*] Do you think we have enough ice?

JACQ: Plenty.

NAOMI: How many people did you invite?

JACQ: About a dozen. But some will bring friends.

NAOMI: Just uni people?

JACQ: Mainly. That's nice.

NAOMI: Thanks. It's not really your kind of thing, though.

JACQ: Well, it's not black. [*She holds a brooch to her chest.*] What do you think?

NAOMI: Yeah, that's good.

JACQ: Dan made this for me. In lapidary club, at school.

NAOMI: What's a lapidary club?

DAN: It's when you hide in the basement at lunch time polishing rocks. Years later people repay you by wearing it, talking about it.

NAOMI: Rock polishing.

DAN: I don't do it any more.

NAOMI: It's nice. You finished in the bathroom?

JACQ: Yeah.

> NAOMI *leaves.*

Dan: Look, I know things didn't go well with the pesto, and I think we both know I'll be the only one here tonight who's recently been in a lapidary club. So maybe we could keep it quiet.

JACQ: You're a little edgy at the moment, I'm sensing.

DAN: I'm the loser who makes food out of dirt, remember? I'm the loser who goes underground at lunchtime to polish rocks. Maybe I should just wear my school uniform to this party and stop pretending I won't be out of place!

JACQ: Dan. Are we going to need a paper bag for you to breathe into? Everything's cool. You'll be fine. You just need to be loose.

DAN: Fine, yeah, sure .

> *She grabs his shoulders.*

JACQ: You'll be fine. Now come on, think loose. You're not thinking loose.

DAN: I'm thinking loose.

JACQ: Imagine the music of the rain forest.

DAN: Music of the rain forest?

JACQ: Whatever. As long as it's loose. Come on. That's better. Now I promise not to mention pesto or lapidary again. But I'm wearing the broach because I like it. And yes, you did make it.

DAN: Please.

JACQ: Loose. You did make it because you're into folk art. Folk art is cool. The kind of men who have their own pesto recipes are into folk art. They wear small steel-framed glasses and natural fibers and gaze into the middle distance with an unresolved inner hurt.

DAN: These are complex men.

JACQ: Oh yes. And very attractive.

DAN: And they probably know some scientific names for trees and birds.

JACQ: They probably do. But it takes time.

DAN: I don't even have the inner hurt yet.

JACQ: Neither do they. They're only faking it.

DAN: So how do I deal with tonight?

JACQ: I don't know. But 16 is too young for a mid-life crisis.

DAN: Could you tell Naomi lapidary's pretty much like folk art?

JACQ: I could do that.

> CHRIS *enters. He has a plastic container, a bedroll and pale spots on his face.*

CHRIS: Hi.

JACQ: Hello Chris.

CHRIS: Can I dump this here?

DAN: Sure.

> JACQ *moves away.*

CHRIS: It wasn't so easy to get here. I think my mother was thinking it was a different kind of party and I had to go with that.

> DAN *opens the plastic container.*

DAN: Butterfly cakes.

CHRIS: I tried to think of another name in the car, but there's no point, I know.

DAN: It could've been worse. It could've been fairy bread.

CHRIS: Don't.

DAN: So when was the last time someone who turned up to a party with butterfly cakes, scored? In the same calendar year?

CHRIS: Sometime before World War One.

DAN: And it's such a different world now.

CHRIS: I'm aware.

DAN: Let's see if Jacq'd like one.

CHRIS: Let's not.

DAN: No, let's. Jacq! Jacq!

CHRIS: You're dead, Banger.

DAN: Look, Chris brought some party food.

JACQ: How nice. And look, they've got little flaps on them. What are they called?

> *Pause.*

DAN: Chris? Do they have a name?

CHRIS: Butterfly cakes.

JACQ: Butterfly cakes. And did you make them yourself?

CHRIS: No.

> CHRIS *walks away.*

JACQ: Things okay now? For you?

DAN: Better.

JACQ: I thought so.

> JACQ *goes into the house with the cakes.* DAN *rejoins* CHRIS.

DAN: The evening begins now. And you never saw those things before. I think that's how we should play it. So it's good you arrived early.

CHRIS: Thanks. And I might wash my face too.

DAN: And wash all that pink stuff off?

> NAOMI *comes in with a butterfly cake.*

CHRIS: My mother jumped me in the car. I'd rather have the zits.

> CHRIS *goes off.*

NAOMI: Hey, these are great. Like retro kid's party food.

DAN: Yeah, cool, hey?

NAOMI: Are you going to have a good time tonight?

DAN: I don't know.

NAOMI: It's your party too you know. You live here.

DAN: I guess. What about you? What are you hoping for?

NAOMI: Music, we need music. I'm going to have a great time.

> NAOMI *leaves.* DAN *frowns. The lights dim. There's music.* CHRIS *comes in with beers.*

CHRIS: Is that still your first?

DAN: Yeah.

CHRIS: I'm on my third.

DAN: I think you should pace yourself.

CHRIS: This is brilliant, hey?

DAN: It's good.

CHRIS: And dark. My parents always keep the lights on.

DAN: Mine too.

CHRIS: I think I like it.

DAN: In this light do you think I'd pass as 21?

CHRIS: Absolutely. Did you see that babe with the black top?

JACQ *comes out, puts her arms around the boys.*

DAN: Which one?

JACQ: So, you're having a good time?

DAN: Not this black T-shirt?

CHRIS: No. But now you mention it.

DAN: Don't even think it.

CHRIS: Great party, Jacq.

CHRIS *leaves.*

JACQ: What was that about?

DAN: Nothing. Have you seen Naomi?

JACQ: She was dancing on the front veranda last time I noticed.

DAN *moves to go.*

Dan. It's a party. You're going to have to deal with it.

DAN: What?

JACQ: Whoever she's with, or ends up with, if anyone. It's possible.

DAN: No, I was just… you know. Well.

JACQ: It's hard, isn't it?

DAN: Yeah.

JACQ: But there's lots of people here. You never know your luck.

DAN: What about you? What about your luck?

JACQ: I have low expectations.

DAN: You just need to be loose. Are you thinking loose?

JACQ: Thanks Dan.

DAN: Like you said, there's a lot of people here. You never know your luck.

PHIL: [*offstage*] Jacqueline.

JACQ: Ah, no.

PHIL *comes in, carrying half a carton of beer, wearing shorts, trainers, a short-sleeved shirt and a bright floral tie.*

PHIL: How are you? And Daniel. This is certainly a great party.

JACQ: How are you, Phil?

PHIL: Excellent. Might I put these in the fridge?

JACQ: There's ice in the bathtub.

PHIL: Excellent. Excellent. I don't actually drink myself. I've got an enzyme thing. but I thought I'd bring it for the party.

JACQ: Thanks. That's great. But you'll have one, won't you? It is a party.

PHIL: I really shouldn't.

> DAN *wanders out on to the veranda.* IMOGEN *comes out during the following and stands, sucking a Chuppa-Chup and watching him. He doesn't notice her.*

JACQ: For me, Phil? Just the one for me.

PHIL: Of course. But I'll have to take it slowly.

JACQ: Come and meet some people.

PHIL: Is this light not working? Should I come 'round and fix it?

JACQ: No, it's fine. Party atmosphere.

PHIL: Right. Good idea.

> PHIL *and* JACQ *leave.*

IMOGEN: Hey, are you looking at me?

> DAN *turns.*

Are looking at me?

DAN: I don't think so.

IMOGEN: I think you were.

DAN: No, I think that was someone else.

IMOGEN: And if it was?

DAN: And if it was, what?

IMOGEN: If it was someone else?

DAN: Well, I don't know.

IMOGEN: No, you wouldn't. [*She dabs him with the Chuppa-Chup.*] You wouldn't. [*She peers at him.*] Oh, you are someone else.

DAN: Am I?

IMOGEN: I thought you were someone else. I'm sorry. A guy I was talking to before. Sorry.

DAN: That's okay.

IMOGEN: No it's not. [*She drops the Chuppa-Chup.*] Shit. Hey want a Chuppa-Chup? I was at this party earlier and they had a bowl-full. I've got more. I'm not going to give you this one because someone's sucked it. So have I. I'm Imogen.

DAN: Hi, I'm Dan, Daniel, Dan.

IMOGEN: That's a bit complicated. Can I just call you Dan?

DAN: Dan is fine.

> *Pause.*

IMOGEN: I'm sorry.

DAN: Why?

IMOGEN: You know. I'm not very good at this. This is, well, pretty much my first uni party. Second actually, but the other one was before. With the Chuppa-Chups. And I don't really know anyone.

DAN: Me neither.

IMOGEN: Yeah? I just started uni, right, so I've only been there a week. So don't ask me anything because I wouldn't know. It's hard though, fitting in. Did you find it hard when you first started uni?

DAN: You get used to it.

> *Pause.*

IMOGEN: So, are you a friend of Nigel's?

DAN: Who's Nigel?

IMOGEN: He was in this book I read. For when you can't think of anything to say. You can talk about the cat, or transport or ask if they're a friend of Nigel.

DAN: And Nigel was what, the host or something?

IMOGEN: He was just in the bloody book, okay?

DAN: Right. I don't think I know him.

IMOGEN: Me neither. I don't know anyone. I should go home. I'm just embarrassing myself. I shouldn't be here.

DAN: Yes you should. It's a party. You're as welcome as anyone.

IMOGEN: I think I'll go home.

DAN: Imogen. You'll be fine, really. Don't go.

IMOGEN: Thanks, Dan. You're nice. Did you find it hard coming to parties at first?

DAN: Yeah, but they're okay. You just need to be loose. I mean you think that everyone else is on top of it but they're not really. Or that everyone's into interesting things.

IMOGEN: And you think they know so much.

DAN: Like the scientific names of trees and birds.

IMOGEN: Exactly.

DAN: And some people do, but so what. Everyone knows different things.

IMOGEN: So what about you?

DAN: What about me?

IMOGEN: What do you do at uni?

DAN: Law, QUT, second year.

IMOGEN: Oh right.

DAN: Gardens Point campus. The parking sucks.

IMOGEN: It must be bad. That's what the other guy said. You probably know him. His name was, um, Chris. He's doing second-year law too. I didn't like him. Do you like him?

DAN: I don't think I know him.

IMOGEN: Really. You're doing the same course?

DAN: There's a lot of people I don't know. We're divided up into groups.

IMOGEN: For tutes and things?

DAN: Yeah.

IMOGEN: Well you wouldn't want to know this Chris…

DAN: Burns.

IMOGEN: I thought you didn't know him?

DAN: I must have heard his name somewhere. I think I saw it on a list.

IMOGEN: And you remembered?

DAN: Yeah. I think he's the only Chris in our year.

IMOGEN: Really? How many Imogens?

JACQ: [*entering*] It's all my fault.

DAN: What?

JACQ: Have one for me, I said. Just one beer.

IMOGEN *slips away.*

Now Phil is dancing on the sofa in his underpants.

DAN: At least he's not still wearing the tie.

JACQ: Underpants, shoes, socks and tie, I should have said.

DAN: I did hear some cheering.

JACQ: I left when he flicked his singlet in my direction.

DAN: A definite gesture of affection, I'd say.

JACQ: Well…

PHIL: [*entering*] There you are, Jacqueline!

JACQ: Phil. Go back inside. Put your clothes on.

PHIL: Not until you say you love me.

JACQ: Don't be ridiculous.

PHIL: But I love you.

JACQ: Phil, get inside!

PHIL: No. I want the world to know. [*He charges into the back yard.*] I love Jacqueline!

JACQ: Phil, stop being stupid.

PHIL: I love Jacqueline.

> *And he runs off still shouting.*

DAN: I think we know why he's so keen to come 'round and fix things.

JACQ: Yeah, I think we do. I had no idea.

DAN: I said your luck would change.

JACQ: Even my lowest expectations were higher than that. I need a drink.

> JACQ *leaves.* DAN *looks around, then wanders into the yard.*

DAN: Naomi?

NAOMI: Hey, lapidary guy.

DAN: I'm way past that now.

NAOMI: And we all have things we want to put behind us, don't we?

DAN: We do. Especially Phil.

NAOMI: [*laughing*] Especially Phil. Poor Jacq.

DAN: So why aren't you in there partying?

NAOMI: I was sort of hoping Jason would turn up tonight. Which is stupid. I'm not even sure that I liked him, you know. I deserve better, according to Jacq.

DAN: I would agree.

NAOMI: Thanks.

DAN: You deserve… the best.

NAOMI: Thanks Dan. You're all right, you know that?

> *She puts her arm around him.*

DAN: And so are you.

> JACQ *and* CHRIS *come out.*

JACQ: There you are. This is our party, you don't have to hide in the backyard. Come and dance.

NAOMI: [*to* DAN] Come and dance with me.

> *They move to go inside, but* CHRIS, *now very drunk, grabs* DAN. JACQ *and* NAOMI *leave.*

CHRIS: Banger. How is this, hey? How is this?

DAN: It's good. I'll talk to you in a minute.

> *But* CHRIS *has him by the arm.*

CHRIS: Come on, it's excellent. Yeah? Excellent. I've met all these excellent people. Like that Danish girl. Did you meet the Danish girl? I don't think she spoke much English. But she's gone now. Did you meet her?

DAN: No.

CHRIS: Mate, you're not circulating. You won't meet anyone if you hide out here. Am I right?

DAN: So let me go inside, okay.

CHRIS: This Dan, this… is a party…

DAN: I noticed.

CHRIS: So you've gotta party. Am I right?

DAN: You're right.

> IMOGEN *come out.* CHRIS *punches* DAN *and is about to leave when he has a thought.*

CHRIS: Remember, second-year Law, QUT.

DAN: Right.

CHRIS: [*to* IMOGEN] I think you should come and dance with me.

IMOGEN: No, I don't think so.

CHRIS: Suit yourself.

> CHRIS *leaves.*

IMOGEN: Hey, Nigel. You met the other QUT guy.

DAN: I did.

IMOGEN: Isn't this such a good party?

DAN: Excellent.

IMOGEN: That girl, with the black top, is she your girlfriend?

DAN: Jacq? No. Why did you think that?

IMOGEN: No, I just wondered.

DAN: She's just a friend.

IMOGEN: Do you like my hair?

DAN: Ah, yeah.

IMOGEN: But the colour. What about the colour?

DAN: I like it. Did you dye it?

IMOGEN: Yeah.

DAN: What colour was it before?

IMOGEN: Black.

DAN: But it's black now.

IMOGEN: Yeah, but it's a different shade of black.

DAN: I'm not sure you've really got black worked out.

IMOGEN: I just wanted to dye it.

DAN: Whereas brown, now brown has a lot of different shades. As many as 48. Maybe more. But black's pretty absolute, really.

IMOGEN: But you like it?

DAN: Sure.

IMOGEN: I'm glad you like it.

> *She throws her arms around him and they both stand there swaying for a moment until she lifts her head from his shoulder and they kiss. Freeze.* DAN *ducks out from under her arms.* IMOGEN *stays frozen.*

DAN: Dan, you're kissing a girl on the mouth. You have definitely passed the conversation phase and moved on. Kissing a girl and I'm pretty sure this isn't a fantasy. Amazing. You should stop watching this and be part of it. And now what? Be cool, Dan. Be cool. Take it slow.

> DAN *steps back into the embrace.* IMOGEN *unfreezes.*

IMOGEN: I'm sorry.

DAN: No, that was nice.

IMOGEN: Yeah?

DAN: Real good.

> *They begin to kiss again as* JACQ *comes in. They stop.* JACQ *smiles and leaves, not wanting to interrupt.* DAN *goes to kiss her again.*

IMOGEN: I'm sorry, it's a bit public.

DAN: Yeah, it is a bit.

> IMOGEN *looks around and grabs his hand.*

IMOGEN: Come on. In here.

> *And she takes him into his own room.*

Do you think they'll mind.

DAN: I'm pretty confident it'll be fine.

IMOGEN: It's good that it's dark.

DAN: Very good.

> *They fall onto the bed,* IMOGEN *on top of* DAN. *They kiss for a moment before* IMOGEN *sits up and removes her top.*

IMOGEN: There's something I should tell you.

DAN: What?

> *And he runs his hand down over her stomach.*

IMOGEN: Oh, don't.

DAN: Sorry.

IMOGEN: Don't touch my stomach.

DAN: No, sorry.

IMOGEN: It's just… I'm a bit… I'm a bit…

> *And she throws up on him.*

Oh, God.

> DAN *crawls from under her, passes her the wastepaper bin and wipes himself with a T-shirt.* IMOGEN *throws up into the bin.*

Oh, God, Dan… I'm sorry.

DAN: You'll be okay.

> *He pats her on the back.*

IMOGEN: Ah… I'm so sorry. I'm so embarrassed.

DAN: Don't be.

IMOGEN: I have to go home.

DAN: Hey, it doesn't matter. I'll get you some water.

IMOGEN: I think I should find my sister. She'll take me home.

DAN: Come into the bathroom and clean up.

IMOGEN: I just feel stupid.

DAN: Don't. Don't feel stupid. Because you're not.

IMOGEN: Oh Dan… [*She starts to cry.*] I have to go.

> IMOGEN *leaves. Music and lights fade. The morning sun rises on* DAN *sitting on* CHRIS*'s bedroll where he has slept, and* CHRIS *asleep on the bed.* JACQ *is on the veranda with a plastic bottle of water.* DAN *gets up and looks at the chaos. He picks a few things up including his essay, which he drops in the bin.*

DAN: I'm sorry my essay is late, sir. I had a half-naked uni student in my room and she threw up on it.

> DAN *sits at his desk.*

CHRIS: [*in his sleep*] Huuuuuh.

DAN: Are you still alive there?

CHRIS: Butterfly cakes.

> *Followed by some choking noises.*

DAN: Hello, Mrs Burns. Yeah, it's Dan. Just thought I'd let you know Chris won't be home, he choked to death on his own vomit. [DAN *leaves his room. Seeing* JACQ.] You're up.

JACQ: I am.

> *She passes him the water.*

DAN: Thanks.

JACQ: So, what did you think of last night?

DAN: Strange but good.

JACQ: I have a vague memory of seeing you with some girl. Dark hair. Was that you?

DAN: Could've been.

JACQ: Three lonely people yearning after those they can't have. And you're the one who gets lucky. Why is that?

> DAN *grins. Pause.*

DAN: Who are you yearning after?

JACQ: You know.

DAN: No. Not really.

JACQ: I thought you did.

DAN: No.

JACQ: You don't have a clue, do you?

DAN: Jacq, what is this?

JACQ: Sorry. Sorry, Dan. I'm… this is not that easy.

DAN: Have I done something?

JACQ: No, no. It's not you. There's some stuff I'm still working out. Naomi in there.

DAN: I'm sorry about the Naomi situation. I wish I could handle it better. I'm so obvious. It's embarrassing.

JACQ: Obvious is not necessarily a bad thing. Better than the way I've been playing it.

DAN: Playing what?

JACQ: How I feel about Naomi.

DAN: How *you* feel about Naomi?

JACQ: Yeah.

DAN: Oh, my God.

> *Pause.*

Right. I'm up with the idea now.

JACQ: What are you thinking?

DAN: Does she know?

JACQ: I'm not even sure she know how you feel about her, so I doubt it.

DAN: So what do we do?

JACQ: What do we do? I suppose we arm wrestle and then go and tell her who won.

DAN: Loser gets Chris.

JACQ: These are high stakes.

DAN: So what happens?

JACQ: Probably nothing. I mean we shouldn't get carried away with the idea that we're competing here.

DAN: Do either of us have a chance?

JACQ: I doubt it. I certainly don't.

DAN: At least you didn't make pesto. You're not so transparent.

JACQ: To me maybe. But Naomi's kind of detached. And don't get too stressed about the pesto. She doesn't know about it and it would've been good without the dirt.

DAN: Is that supposed to be encouraging?

JACQ: Yeah. I'm guessing you'll leave the dirt out next time.

DAN: Next time?

JACQ: What, you'd give up after one go?

DAN: I guess not.

JACQ: Listen, this is a bit of a surprise to me, too. I've had a sense of things being not quite right, but, I suppose I thought it would go away. And then I broke up with that guy last year, and really, it wasn't him, I was starting to go crazy, so I ended it. And since then I've been thinking about why. And then Naomi came along. I must be still drunk, telling you all this.

DAN: No, it's good to talk.

JACQ: I didn't know what you'd think.

DAN: What is there to think? It's not really anything to do with me.

JACQ: Correct me if I'm wrong, but aren't we both lusting after the same person? Some things are to do with you, Dan.

DAN: No, look, sorry. I didn't mean about Naomi. I mean about how you feel, about… well, life… generally.

JACQ: And how is that exactly?

DAN: You know what I mean. The, ah, orientation thing.

JACQ: Lesbian is the word you're avoiding.

DAN: Could be.

JACQ: Oh, my Gahd.

DAN: Yeah, sorry. You took me by surprise. It doesn't mean I have a problem. I'd say the same thing if I won Lotto.

NAOMI: [*entering*] I've made some coffee. Want some?

JACQ: Please.

DAN: That'd be good.

NAOMI: Two sugars and one sugar.

JACQ: One sugar.

DAN: Two sugars.

NAOMI: Yeah. Right.

      NAOMI *leaves.*

JACQ: She has the memory of a pencil case. But you've got to love her.

DAN: You do.

JACQ: I'm glad I told you first.

DAN: Thanks. So am I. I've never been told anything first before.

JACQ: I'm sorry this is all so weird. It's probably not the year you were expecting.

DAN: It's more interesting than calculus.

JACQ: Tell me one thing. There was only ever maths calculus, wasn't there?

DAN: Only maths.

JACQ: That's what I thought. Should we clean up? Or should we just move.

DAN: Move. That way I don't have to deal with my room.

JACQ: Is it ugly?

DAN: Various people, not including me, were throwing up in there last night.

NAOMI: [*entering with coffee*] The kitchen is disgusting.

JACQ: Apparently Dan's room is worse.

NAOMI: And what was happening in your room that you ended up sleeping on my bed?

JACQ: I don't want to know. But there was some kind of action happening in the dark.

NAOMI: But not for you, hey? Still sticking to the no-man rule?

JACQ: Pretty much.

NAOMI: What about you, Dan?

DAN: I'm on a no-man rule myself.

NAOMI: Hello, basil, how are you this morning, darling?

DAN: I'm very thirsty.

NAOMI: You poor thing. I'll get you some water.

> NAOMI *leaves.*

JACQ: I nearly told her last night. But I'm glad I didn't. Come on. Cleaning time.

> JACQ *leaves.* DAN *goes to his bedroom where* CHRIS *is gathering his things.*

CHRIS: Great party.

DAN: Yeah.

CHRIS: Sorry about the bed. I can't believe I threw up that much.

DAN: Someone else threw up.

CHRIS: I'm pretty sure it was me.

DAN: Someone else, as well as you.

CHRIS: You?

DAN: No, a girl called Imogen.

CHRIS: I had a girl in here? I don't remember. Imogen. Dark hair. Yeah.
And I got her into bed? Did I… you know?

DAN: Well, something made her throw up.

CHRIS: Wow.

DAN: You can borrow some clothes if you want. What about your
clothes, do you want a garbage bag?

CHRIS: I'll roll it all up in the sleeping bag. What's my mother going
to say?

DAN: If only you knew how to use the washing machine.

CHRIS: Life is so complicated.

DAN: Oh, yeah.

> CHRIS *leaves.* DAN *goes to* NAOMI *who is watering the basil.*

NAOMI: Hey, the basil's growing. We'll be able to use it soon. Do you
like pesto?

DAN: Yeah, I've got a recipe for pesto. Not that I've ever made any.

NAOMI: Did I see you with a girl last night?

DAN: I spoke to lots of people.

NAOMI: This one had her arms around you.

DAN: Oh, that one.

NAOMI: Is someone's luck about to change around here?

DAN: I don't think so. Not mine anyway.

NAOMI: Why not? Didn't you like her?

DAN: She threw up on me.

NAOMI: Aw yuck.

DAN: And all over my bed.

NAOMI: I'm sure she didn't mean to.

DAN: No, but it meant that she left pretty quickly, and I really don't
know who she was. Do you know her?

NAOMI: Not one of my friends.

DAN: I suppose we should clean up.

> DAN *sits on the veranda with a letter and postcard.*

JACQ: [*entering*] You answering your mum's letter?

DAN: Yeah.

JACQ: Oh, we got another letter today. Sad news.

> *The letter is next to the phone. She reads from it.*

Dear tenants, I refer to the above property. From this date, this property will be managed by the property management division of LJ Hooker Toowong on behalf of the owner Phillip John Borthwick. A copy of the authorisation to act as agent for Mr Borthwick is enclosed. Please contact this office if you have any questions about the property or your tenancy, or if maintenance is required at any time.

DAN: Or if he wants his clothes back.

JACQ: That probably comes under questions about the property.

DAN: You're missing him already, aren't you?

JACQ: Poor Phil. But who am I to be smug about falling in love with the wrong people.

DAN: Our friend the bird.

DAN *makes bird noises at it.*

JACQ: And what have you been telling Naomi?

DAN: Nothing. I didn't say anything. She must have figured it out herself.

JACQ: What?

DAN: We haven't been talking about you at all.

JACQ: But she knows?

DAN: Isn't that what you're saying?

JACQ: I was talking about the bird.

DAN: Oh, right, sorry. Nothing to do with you then.

JACQ: No. Glad we cleared that up. I was talking about how Naomi's taken to calling it Bill. Because Striated Thornbill's too long. Call it a wild guess, but I think you're involved.

DAN: Maybe.

JACQ: Any idea what striated means?

DAN: Not really.

JACQ: Thought not. Nor does Naomi obviously. What are the two of you on about?

DAN: Don't worry. I think I've learned my lesson. So I've got a new plan.

JACQ: Yeah, tell me.

DAN: A do-nothing plan.

JACQ: That is so much better than I was expecting.

DAN: The plans keep going wrong. From now on, they're going to have to come to me. They're going to have to make the moves.

JACQ: That's a lot to expect. But definitely safer.

DAN: Exactly. But I can do the intense gaze into the distance. Watch.

JACQ: You should be killing them with this kind of material. If I wasn't playing with the kids on the other side of the park, and a close blood-relative, who knows. It's no surprise you had a girl in your bed the other night.

DAN: Well, if you need any tips.

JACQ: On what?

DAN: Picking up girls.

> JACQ *punches him.*

Sorry.

JACQ: What are you writing?

DAN: Just the usual postcard.

JACQ: Yeah, but what's it say?

> DAN *picks up the card and pretends to read.*

DAN: Dear Mum, haven't been getting much schoolwork done. There was a party on Saturday and everyone got drunk and threw up and I found out Jacq is a lesbian.

> JACQ *grabs the card. She looks at it, smiles, then reads.*

JACQ: Thanks for the calculus tip. We had a party here on Saturday. Everything's going well at school. Jacq says hi. Love Dan.

> JACQ *beats him with the card.*

I should've asked 300 for you.

DAN: Well, give me a break. As if I'd say anything. I can be trusted you know.

JACQ: Yeah, sorry.

DAN: And if you did tell Mum I think she'd be more understanding than you realize.

JACQ: You think?

DAN: Yeah, I do.

> CHRIS *enters with a carry-bag.*

JACQ: Hi Chris.

CHRIS: Hi.

> JACQ *leaves.*

Sorry about this. But mum made me bring your clothes back. You know what she's like. She's waiting in the car. It was a cool party.

DAN: Not bad, hey.

CHRIS: I probably won't be over again until the holidays, though. My weekend behaviour is apparently not the kind of return my parents expected when they invested in a private school education.

DAN: Invested?

CHRIS: The exact word. I can't believe you've got a whole year without that kind of shit.

DAN: Still, I hear you scored.

CHRIS: Yeah, well…

DAN: In my bed, with a uni student. Eight people at school have mentioned it.

CHRIS: You put up one notice and suddenly everyone knows.

DAN: But it didn't happen.

CHRIS: Are you going to blow it for me?

DAN: Of course not.

CHRIS: Thanks. I better go. [*He notices* DAN*'s essay on the table.*] You got 19-and-a-half out of 20 for this?

DAN: What'd you get?

CHRIS: 16.

DAN: You can't expect to excel at your schoolwork when these uni babes are demanding so much of your time.

CHRIS: That's right. That is so right.

> CHRIS *leaves.* DAN *follows him to the door. Evening.* NAOMI *is on the veranda reading* DAN*'s essay.* DAN *approaches.*

DAN: I wouldn't bother.

> *He tries to take it.*

NAOMI: No, wait.

DAN: I really wouldn't bother.

NAOMI: Just let me finish. If that's okay.

> DAN *lets her finish, uncomfortable as this makes him.*

Oh, it's so sad. And it's there so early on, isn't it, with the fish-tank scene? They are so close, but they can't touch. This is so good.

DAN: Thanks.

NAOMI: I liked the film, and that scene really got to me, but I hadn't thought why. You know it's going to end in disaster. But they don't know. And it seems unfair. And in the film it's that scene that sets it all up.

DAN: The scene got to me too. Because all they knew was there was something on the other side of the fish-tank. Something tantalising and unattainable. But you can walk around a fish-tank, and they met each other soon enough. And it turned out that it was unattainable, and disastrous, but they were too innocent to realize.

NAOMI: There's a lot happening in your head, isn't there?

DAN: Sometimes.

NAOMI: Fish-tank theories, birds.

DAN: I'm not that big on birds, to be truthful.

NAOMI: Yeah, I know.

NAOMI *puts her arm around him. They look at each other.*

JACQ: [*entering*] Hi kids, what's happening?

NAOMI: Reading Dan's essay. He got 19-and-a-half out of 20.

JACQ: Smart boy is our Dan. Anyone want a beer?

NAOMI: Yeah, that'd be good.

DAN: I'll move my stuff. I haven't been getting much study done anyway.

JACQ: I noticed.

DAN *moves to his room.* JACQ *leaves.*

[*offstage*] Any phone calls?

NAOMI: Not since I've been home.

JACQ *returns with the beers and gives one to* NAOMI.

Thanks. Do you think they'd consider fish, pets?

JACQ: Our new agents, you mean?

NAOMI: Yeah. It'd be nice to have a fish-tank, what do you think?

JACQ: Sure.

JACQ *takes the beer to* DAN *in his room.*

DAN: Thanks.

JACQ: Did I just interrupt something there?

DAN: I don't know.

JACQ: So why has she got a sudden interest in fish?

DAN: I don't know, ask her.

JACQ: As if either of us would do anything as straight forward as asking her. I don't understand either of you. I'll leave you to your work.

DAN: There was a phone call for you. Lisa. Something about going to a movie.

JACQ: Right, thanks.

DAN: She's the girl from the band, isn't she?

JACQ: Yeah.

DAN: I saw her at the party, getting pretty intense with some woman in the corner.

JACQ: They've split up since then.

The phone rings. NAOMI *answers it.*

DAN: She seemed nice.

JACQ: We'll see.

NAOMI: [*on phone*] Hello. Yeah, speaking... Matt, yeah it was good seeing you again, too... Yeah, sure, when...? Friday night's good for me... Okay, Matt, see you then.

NAOMI *leaves.*

DAN: Just for a second there...

JACQ: A second. You were in for several minutes. Anyway, I've met Matt. He's a dick. Naomi's great but she has no taste.

DAN: And aren't we living proof of that.

JACQ: Sad but true.

DAN: It's a bad idea anyway. I mean for a second there it seemed actually possible. And suddenly it seemed like a bad idea. I've got to live here with her for the next 12 months.

JACQ: Rule Number One, never get involved with a housemate.

DAN: Actually that's Rule Number Two. Rule Number One is never listen to the advice of Chris Burns.

JACQ: [*laughing*] It's a pity you didn't fancy that girl from the party. She seemed keen. You wouldn't need a plan at all, you could stick to your new do-nothing plan if she was already interested.

DAN: I hadn't thought of that. And I did like her. I thought she was great. But she's at uni, and, you know… but if you run into her…

JACQ: I don't even know who she was, and uni's a big place.

DAN: Imogen. Her name is Imogen.

JACQ: Imogen? You sure? And she was at uni?

DAN: That's what she said.

JACQ: Was she was wearing a green T-shirt?

DAN: That sounds like her.

JACQ: That's Emma's sister. I don't think she's at uni though, I think she's still at school.

DAN: Really?

JACQ: But if she said she was at uni…

DAN: No, no. I might have heard wrong. Do you see Emma, much?

JACQ: Yeah, all the time.

DAN: Well, if you see her…

JACQ: Put in a word?

DAN: But don't mention about school. Just Dan. It's possible she somehow got the idea that I'm in second-year Law at QUT.

JACQ: How would she get that idea?

DAN: Dan or Nigel. She might remember me as Nigel.

JACQ: I'm not even going to ask.

DAN: Thank you.

JACQ: Actually I could do something else. I could go and get my address book and give you her number. Emma still lives at home.

DAN: Then I'd have to ring her up.

JACQ: You would.

DAN: And I'd have some misunderstandings to sort out.

JACQ: Like Law at QUT.

DAN: Yeah, for a start.

JACQ: I'll go and get the number.

> JACQ *leaves.* IMOGEN *is now standing on stage in her school uniform. They smile at each other.*

THE END

TEACHERS' NOTES
by Sandra Gattenhof

TABLE OF CONTENTS

Program Overview   59
Themes and Issues   60
    Structure of the Play   61
    Characters   61
Interview with Playwright Philip Dean   62
Learning Experiences for Students   65
    Drama/English   65
    Human Relationships Education 69
Responding to the Play   71
Resources for Further Development   72
    Resource Sheets   74

PROGRAM OVERVIEW

La Boite Theatre continues its strong relationship with playwright Philip Dean, author of *Long Gone Lonesome Cowgirls, First Asylum* and the successful *After January*, with another adaption of Nick Earls' award-winning novel.

Dan is in his final year of school. His parents have gone overseas and he has moved in with his Aunt Jacq and her friend Naomi. He should be concentrating on calculus but Jacq is 23 and likes to practise her bass guitar playing, and Naomi indulges in loud sex in the next room. For Dan's mate, Chris, this is all too good to be true. But for Dan, it's confusing and distracting. Instead of studying, he finds himself trying to impress Naomi… and she is hard to impress.

This is the second in the series of successful collaborations between Nick Earls and Philip Dean, based on Nick's honest retelling of the rites of passage for young men and Philip's understated theatrical craftsmanship. Combined, they provide for great theatre.

THEMES AND ISSUES

This play explores an adolescent boy's rite of passage into adulthood. Dan is beginning his final year of school with a whole new set of 'adult' responsibilities which have never been a consideration before. Apart from his desire to succeed academically, he suddenly has to learn how to function on all levels in a world without parental influence, support and guidance. During this important time in his life Dan grapples with important adolescent issues of:

- Independence
- Adult responsibilities
- First love and sexual encounters
- Sexual orientation
- Parental relationships.

SUITABILITY

Year levels	Years 10–12.
Language	No coarse language.
Sex	Referred to in the context of a relationship between an adolescent male and female.
Setting	Brisbane, Queensland.

CURRICULUM

Drama	Australian Drama and Student Devised Drama (in relation to transforming other forms into Drama).
English	Queensland author and playwright; transformation of a book of fiction into a play.
Human Relationships Education	Adulthood, relationships with family members and older people, sexual issues and orientation.

STRUCTURE OF THE PLAY

48 Shades of Brown is written as a linear narrative which sequentially follows chronological time. In some sections Dan (the main character which the action revolves around) has 'dream sequences'. These sequences are short and show Dan's forward projections or inner monologues in situations which he finds himself. The action takes place in a share house in the Brisbane suburb of Toowong, a suburb famous for university share houses.

Act One has scenes taking place at Brisbane International Airport, a high school and the Toowong share house. In Act Two scenes take place by the university lakes (Queensland University) and at the Toowong house.

CHARACTERS

Dan, aged 16
  Dan is in his final year of high school. His parents are living and working in Geneva, Switzerland while he stays in Brisbane. He has moved in with his aunt, Jacq. Dan's nickname is 'Banger'.
Jacq, aged 23
  Uni student and Dan's auntie. Jacq is the sister of Dan's mother. She plays bass guitar in an amatuer band.
Naomi, aged 18
  Shares the house with Jacq and is a second-year Psychology student. Naomi has an 'active' sex life.
Imogen, aged 16
  A school student who likes eating Chuppa-Chups. Dan meets Imogen at a party in the house where he is living when she pretends that she is a first-year university student.
Girl
  A character of Dan's imagination.
Clare
  As in Clare Danes, the actress who played the part of Juliet in Baz Luhrmann's film version of *Romeo + Juliet*. Dan is studying the film at school. Clare appears as a figment of his imagination.
Chris, aged 16
  Dan's best mate. He goes to the same school as Dan and is obsessed with girls and talking about sex.

Jason, aged 21
    Boyfriend of Naomi.
Phil, aged 30
    Landlord of Jacq and Naomi's house. He aspires to be a documentary
    maker.
Inga, aged about 16
    A Danish girl. She appears as a figment of Dan's imagination.

INTERVIEW WITH PLAYWRIGHT PHILIP DEAN

*1/ Can you describe the process of adapting a novel into a playscript?
How do you capture the integrity of the original work, while creating
something that is new?*

Philip: Perhaps the most important part in the whole process is my
first reading of the novel. I only get to read it in innocence once. From
then on I have to draw on my memory of what I hoped for as the story
unfolded and how I related to the characters. Once I get down to work
I have to confront the very significant differences between a play and
a novel.

The way a novel is read is controlled by the reader; the way a play is
experienced is controlled by the production. If you miss something in
a play you can't flip back and reread a few pages. The place and clarity
of a play, therefore, need to be carefully considered.

On stage there is only real time. A novelist has an array of devices
to move around in time. 'Earlier', 'later', 'afterwards', or 'now'
frequently begin sentences. On stage it is always now. Nick can write,
'Naomi goes to change for work, and the phone rings when she comes
out of her room'. But no one wants to sit in the theatre staring at the
scenery for three or four minutes while Naomi actually goes off stage to
change. It is necessary therefore to break up the story into a number of
discreet, real-time moments. My script doesn't number these moments
but there are about 25 that run together.

A story that is told in the first person, like 48 Shades, does
present a problem. Characters exist in their own right on stage. First
person narration lets us experience the thoughts and feelings of the
protagonist but it only shows us the other characters through the
eyes of the narrator. Because a play takes place in real space some

incidents are difficult to dramatise. I try to find something that has the same feel but is practical. For instance, in the novel there are several sequences where Dan and Naomi play with a dog. In the play they bounce a basketball.

All of these aspects mean that the experience of seeing the play can never be the same as reading the novel. Nonetheless, if I get it right I can tell Nick's story, keeping something of the tone and texture of the original, in a way that is enjoyable for both those who have read the novel and those who haven't.

2/ How did 48 Shades of Brown *emerge as a playscript? Was it commissioned by La Boite or did you and Nick Earls have the vision of adapting the novel for stage?*

Philip: 48 Shades was commissioned by La Boite. They approached Nick Earls with the idea and when they had his agreement they asked me if I would adapt it.

3/ What type of communication, if any, do you try to have with the novelist and director in the process of adaption?

Philip: Nick has generously handed over his novel and let me get on with it. To the best of my knowledge he was happy with how *After January* came together on the stage and he has trusted me with *48 Shades of Brown*. I hope he likes the final result. I work closely with the director, Jean-Marc Russ, and La Boite's Artistic Director, Sean Mee, having lengthy discussions after each draft. Then when rehearsals begin, I try to be there as much as possible and listen to the feedback from the actors. Theatre is very much a group process.

4/ What appeals to you most about both the original text and the adaption that you have created?

Philip: All of Nick's novels have a wonderful sense of place, something I am forever saying is important in writing. His stories uncover the drama of ordinary people in ordinary situations. His humour is one of recognition and is easy to identify with. The challenge and reward for me is finding the right theatrical language to express these qualities.

5/ In both After January *and* 48 Shades of Brown *you have captured the voice of young people in a very authentic way. As a mature playwright do you ever have difficulty getting into the heads of young people?*

Philip: The job of any writer is to imagine what it would be like to be someone else. In part this is possible because we share common emotions. We might want different things but we all recognise disappointment, embarrassment, panic, lonliness and all the other states of mind that the world imposes upon us. I really don't think there is anything very different in a young head. The only thing you don't know at 16 that you know at 36 is that we don't change very much. We just become more practised and adept. It is only when writers assume that there is something different and weird about being teenage that the result is fake and patronising.

6/ Thinking back over the years, what productions, texts, or other sources have profoundly influenced you as a playwright? How does this inspiration manifest itself in your work?

Philip: I read a lot and whether the author is Sei Shonagon, Jane Austen or Irvine Welsh, they all have their effect. Though having mentioned Jane Austen, I should say that I am a great admirer of hers. It is sometimes said that plot is more important in a play than in a novel, but *Emma*, for example, is better plotted than most plays.

Among playwrights, I particularly admire the Irish writers. Samuel Beckett, Brendan Behan, Brian Friel, Sebastion Barry and Conor McPherson, to pick just a few from a long list, all seem to approach playwriting as though they invented it themselves. They are difficult to learn from because they are so idiosyncratic. But a great play, like *Translations* or *The Steward of Christendom*, inspires me simply because it is great; because it moves and challenges me and I can't get it out of my head. And because it reminds me what an extraordinary experience two hours in a theatre can be.

7/ Over the years there has been much debate over what can be defined as Australian Theatre. For you what constitutes Australian Theatre at the present, in terms of form, style and content?

Philip: I suspect that this issue, like the question of an individual writer's style, is one best left to commentators rather than practitioners. I don't try to write Australian plays, that happens by accident.

LEARNING EXPERIENCES FOR STUDENTS

The following activities support the production of *48 Shades of Brown*. You may like to use these activities in your work with students to investigate issues and themes within the play or to help students formulate responses. They are not in chronological order of development nor are they lesson plans. Instead you may dip in and out and combine them in a way in which you find appropriate for your school.

DRAMA/ENGLISH

Introductions

Each class member is asked to get a small object that belongs to them—preferrably one that does not identify them. The class is asked to walk about the space and as they meet people follow this ritual: Introduce yourself by saying: 'Hi, I'm … and this is my pen', then hand the object to the other person. The other person responds in the same way. Now the objects are swapped between pairs, they continue circulating but now when they greet others they say: 'Hi, I'm … and this is Sally's camera' etc. This continues until the objects are thoroughly distributed. Eventually everyone holds onto whatever object they have and returns to a circle. At this point each person steps into a circle and says: 'Hi, I'm (person's name) and this is a (object) belonging to (owner)'. If the identification is correct, the object is returned to the owner.

Postcards

Divide the class up into roughly two even groups. One group becomes the 'actors' while the other is the 'audience'. Each group will be given multiple opportunities to do both. Provide the acting group with the name of a photograph that relates to experiences they may have encountered as young people (e.g. first day of high school, end of year exams or a school dance). Ask the group, one at a time, to run into the space, take up a frozen image within the photograph, and nominate what they are (e.g. a school desk). The players are not allowed to copy someone else's idea and must watch where people place themselves. To increase the detail in the picture, players may 'tag' onto another person's image (e.g. a book on the school desk). When all the players are in the space and the image is complete count '3, 2, 1… Freeze'. The audience group then takes a snapshot with their imaginary cameras.

Message From Home

In *48 Shades of Brown*, Dan's mother has provided him with a stack of pre-stamped animal postcards—to keep the lines of communication open.

NAOMI: Dan, it's for you. It's your mother.

DAN *goes to the phone.*

DAN: Hello… You didn't say I should call… I just got here… A bit. I'll be alright after a night's sleep… If my plane had crashed you would have seen it on CNN hours ago… Okay… I'll send you an animal postcard… Once a week like we agreed. Everything's fine… Bye. [*He hangs up.*] I didn't think we were doing phone calls. She gave me a stack of pre-paid postcards, but I didn't think we were doing phone calls.

DAN *leaves.*

(pages 6–7)

Ask students to put themselves into Dan's shoes. Ask students in groups to write a list of all the possible events, both positive and negative, that may take place to a young person who finds themself 'out of home' for the very first time. Individually have students select one of these events to write a postcard to their parents about. Once written, ask students to share the postcards in character. Begin with the following postcard from Dan.

DAN: Right! Fine! And thanks, Mum. Thanks for dumping me here and leaving me to deal with all this when I've got my final year of school to worry about. It's not fair, I am never going to fit in here!

(page 13)

Role on the Wall

There are many interesting characters in *48 Shades of Brown* that allow students to delve into character study. In pairs or small groups trace around the outside of a student's body onto a large sheet of paper. Above the outline write the name of the nominated character that the group have been given or chosen to investigate. On the outside of the body-shape, brainstorm all the things they know about the character from the character's own words or actions. On the outside of the body-shape, write all the information known about the character through other characters. When the character studies are complete display them on the wall and discuss each one with the whole group adding and deleting information as necessary.

To take this activity a step further, call for a confident volunteer from each pair/group to take on the role of the character and have them sit in front of the class which can then become a group of journalists. The journalists have the chance to ask the character questions and the character may have to stretch the truth or invent an answer, but must remain true to the character's disposition.

Inner Monologue

Extending on the 'Role on the Wall' activity, ask students to select a character from *48 Shades of Brown*, and then select the most significant moment for that character in the story. Ask the students to write a monolgue that may have been running in the character's mind while the moment was taking place. The character may not have vocalised their thoughts at the time, so ask the students to concentrate on what they were thinking, feeling and responding to. The inner monologe may be a humorous or a dramatic reaction to the event/moment. Once these have been written the students can then share their monologues in small or class groups. Ask the students to consider the following before reading: read it aloud as though they are in character, take on the attitudes/values of the character, use their voice to enhance the character.

Seduction

Divide the class up into teams of four players. Provide each group with a situation in which someone in the team must be seduced by a person or an idea. The seduction can be mental or physical (e.g. convincing a vegetarian to eat meat; getting a teetotaller to drink wine). Beware the scene doesn't become overtly sexual as it will become boring. Allow teams time to create a one-minute improvisation of the seduction. Remember the storyline is of the upmost importance. The event— the seduction—occurs as part of the action. Share the one-minute improvisations with the class.

Emotions
Again, divide the class up into teams of four players. Players are given a situation and two opposing emotions (e.g. on a ferris wheel—love/hate). Players, either with rehearsal time or spontaneously, develop a one-minute scene in which the transition of the emotion is the important event of the scene and must occur for a specific reason found within the scene. Players must 'play' the emotions truthfully. Players can all begin with the same emotion and then all change to the opposing emotion—begin with opposite emotions and swap them during the scene.

Ways into the Text
(This activity was part of a unit of work titled 'Finding a Context: A Study of Youth in Australian Drama' developed by Craig Timms of Somerville House.)
a) Photocopy Resource Sheets 1, 2, 3 and 4 (found at the back of this book).
b) Participants work within small groups (depending on the number of characters in the script extract). They read the extracts provided, and then take notes on what they have discovered about the 'world' in which Dan lives—both denotatively and connotatively.
c) Each group then shares their findings in a series of frozen images. These images can be literal or symbolic. Give each image a title and then share with the class group.
d) Taking the information that has been conveyed through the images, the whole group then constructs a machine titled 'Dan's World'. Each member creates their part of the machine, one at a time, using movement and sound.
e) Participants return back to the small groups, and develop an improvisation that begins and ends the selected piece of text. Each devised part should last approximately one minute.
f) Participants share their works.
   You may like to take this a step further by joining the pieces chronologically with linking devices such as sound, movement, music (perhaps John Lennon's *Nobody Told Me),* or factual information about share houses, young people, 'Houses To Share' advertisements from the accomodation section of the newspaper.

HUMAN RELATIONSHIPS EDUCATION

My Cultural World

Dan's worldview shifts as a result of the new experiences he has living with his Aunt Jacq. The one thing that remains constant is school. For most young people schools are an important cultural icon—they work and socialise, dream and realise in schools. The other places of significance are home and places to hang out with friends. This activity was part of a unit of work titled 'Finding a Context: A Study of Youth in Australian Drama' developed by Craig Timms of Somerville House.

a) Roll out a large sheet of newsprint or pieces of butcher's paper taped together. Ask each student to gather around the paper. Have a selection of art media in the room: paints, crayons, felt pens, coloured pencils, magazines, scissors, glue, staplers, tape.

   Invite the students to use any media that they wish to create an image of their world—it may be symbolic or literal and may contain words. At this point do not censor the work, as it belongs purely to the student. Allow ample time for students to design and create their individual images. Once the mural is complete hang the artwork in the room. Allow students silent time to survey the work. Invite volunteers to share their work with the group.

b) Before the next session, ask the students to bring a symbol of their world to the lesson. Video each student discussing their symbol and its significance in front of the group mural.

c) Replay the video and have the class analyse the segments for commonalities between 'the symbols of youth'.

d) Encourage the students in groups to formulate a response in their chosen form—written, oral, use of drama/movement or a combination. Groups then share their devised work.

The New Pioneers

In the early 1990s, Australian social commentator Hugh MacKay described young people as 'the new pioneers'. He referred to them as the 'first navigators'—the first generation who were required to make sense of a multicultural, postmodern society. French theorist Henri Giroux similiarly referred to young people of the 1990s as 'navigators'.

Richer, 2000: 5

Using this quote as a starting point, engage in a discussion about navigating as a young person in their community/society. Using the metaphor of 'the new pioneers', ask students to visually map out their life—where they have been and where they would like to be heading. Once the map is complete have the students develop a SWOT (Strengths, Weaknesses, Opportunities and Threats) analysis of themselves which will clarify for them what tools they have for navigation now and in the future.

LIFE MAP OF ....

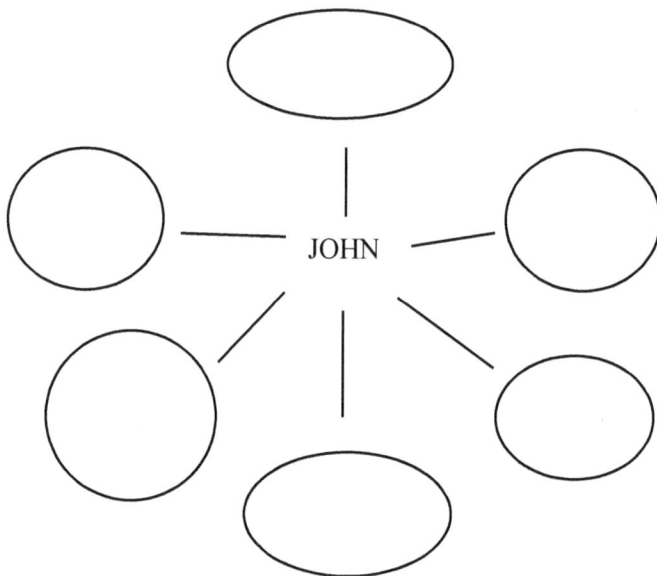

Example of 'The New Pioneer' Map

SWOT ANALYSIS OF ME

STRENGTHS	WEAKNESSES	OPPORTUNITIES	THREATS

Advertising and Sexuality
In the slick world of advertising, teenage bodies are sought after for the exchange value they generate in marketing an adolescent sexuality that offers marginal exoticism and ample pleasures.
Giroux, 1998: 39

Have a variety of magazines available for student use—teen mags, surfing mags, mainstream mags (*New Idea, Woman's Day*), fashion mags. Have a magazine hunt for images of young people that have been used to sell a product or promote a message. Display these images on a wall and divide the class into groups of three of four. Have groups choose one of the images on display to analyse using the following questions as a guide:

- How is the young person being portrayed?
- At what market or target audience is the advertisement aimed?
- What message do advertisers want to give to the market?
- Does the image of a young person suit the product?
- How would you describe the image—exploitive, realistic or voyueristic? Justify your group's response.
- Would you be influenced by this group's advertising? Why/ why not?

Finally, once sharing of the responses has occurred, as a group analyse the images for gender. What is the predominant gender and age used in marketing? What does this say about our values and the values of the broader society?

RESPONDING TO THE PLAY
Revisiting the Elements of Drama is useful to help you discuss *48 Shades of Brown*. A homework or in-class worksheet can be constructed from the following questions to guide response to the play.

1. As a young person which images or moments from the play do you make a connection with?
2. Are there any aspects of the play you find less effective?
3. Describe styles of presentation that could be used by a director and actors in a production of the play.
4. What period of time does the action in the play span? How could this be indicated?
5. What symbols could be used in the production?
6. Consider the staging. What different places and time periods could be suggested by the set?
7. How could music and sound effects be used to enhance a production?
8. Describe the use of language (both verbal and non-verbal) used by the characters. How does language define them?
9. Describe how young people are represented in *48 Shades of Brown*.

RESOURCES FOR FURTHER DEVELOPMENT
In Print

Boal, A. *Games for Actors and Non-Actors*. London: Routledge, 1992.

Contact Youth Theatre. 'By whom, for whom, about whom!': report National Youth Performing Arts Conference, 20–22 April 1990. Maroochydore Queensland. Brisbane: Contact Youth Theatre.

Davis, M. *gangland: cultural elites and the new generationalism*. St Leonards, NSW: Allen & Unwin, 1997.

Giroux, H. 'Teenage sexuality, body politics, and the pedagogy of display' in J.S. Epstein (ed). *Youth Culture—Identity in a Postmodern World*. Massachusetts: Blackwell, 1998.

Lawson, S., Cavallo, C. and Reid, T. 'Let's exchange stories' in *QADIE Says: Hands On Drama*. Vol. 22 No. 4. Brisbane: *QADIE*, 1999, pp.24–28.

Richer, S. 'Navigation and self narration—key points for working with young people in the arts' in *YAQ Papers—Working From the Ground Up, An Exploration of Grounded Aesthetics in Youth Arts and Cultural Development*. Vol. 2 No. 2. Brisbane: Youth Arts Queensland, 2000, pp.5–9.

Stinson, M. and Elmes, S. 'A sense of belonging—a process drama' in *QADIE Says: ARTnerships*. Vol. 22 No. 2. Brisbane: *QADIE*, 2000, pp.36–41.

Turnbull, N. *The Millenium Edge: Prospering with Generation MM*. Sydney: Allen & Unwin, 1996.

Wyn, J. and White, R. *Rethinking Youth*. Sydney: Allen & Unwin, 1997.

Other Plays Which Explore and Support Young People's Personal Experience

Davis, Page, adapted from the novel by Tim Winton. *Lockie Leonard Human Torpedo*. Sydney: Currency Press, 1996.

Davis. Stephen. *Blurred: Created Performances for Young People*. 1999.

Davis, Stephen. *Juice*. 1998.

Dean, Philip, adapted from the novel by Nick Earls. *After January*. Sydney: Currency Press, 2000.

Enright, Nick. *Blackrock*. Sydney: Currency Press, 1996.

Forde, Margery. *X-stacy*. Sydney: Currency Press, 1999.

Fry, Garry, adapted from the novel by Tim Winton. *Lockie Leonard Scumbuster.* Sydney: Currency press, 2000.

Morris, Mary, adapted from the novel by Morris Gleitzman. *Two Weeks with the Queen*. Sydney: Currency Press, 1993.

Robinson, Sancia and Harmer, Wendy. *What's the matter with Mary Jane?* Sydney: Currency Press, 1996.

Organisations

YOUTH ARTS QUEENSLAND
Level 3, 420 Brunswick Street, Fortitude Valley Qld 4006
phone: 07 3252 5115
email: info@yaq.org.au
website: http://www.yaq.org.au

BACKBONE YOUTH ARTS
Level 3, Metro Arts, 109 Edward Street, Brisbane Qld 4000
phone: 07 3210 2666
email: info@backbone.org.au
website: http://www.backbone.org.au

DRAMA QUEENSLAND
PO Box 215, Paddington Qld 4064
fax: 07 3009 0059
email: admin@dramaqueensland.org.au
website: http://www.dramaqueensland.org.au

Information and support is also available from services including:
KIDS' HELP LINE
Tollfree: 1800 55 1800
website: http://www.kidshelp.com.au/ Includes infosheets, research,
newsletters and resources.

Community Health Services, e.g. Child and Adolescent Mental Health
Services, Women's Health Centres, Aboriginal and Torres Strait
Islanders' Health Services.

*

Teachers' Notes Writer—Sandra Gattenhof, with thanks to Philip
Dean, Rosemary Herbert and Katrina Torenbeek.

*

RESOURCE SHEET 1
From *48 Shades of Brown*:

NAOMI: Dan, this is Jason.
DAN: Hi.
JASON: So you've just moved in, yeah?
DAN: Today.
JASON: You in first-year?
NAOMI: No, this is Jacq's... ah...
DAN: Nephew.
NAOMI: That means she's your aunt. Weird.

DAN: My mother's 21 years older than Jacq.

NAOMI: Are they alike? I haven't met your mother.

DAN: You have, I think. When she was moving my stuff in.

NAOMI: That was your mother?

JASON: So who else would it have been? Did you just think he liked older women, or something?

NAOMI: We passed on the steps. I didn't think about it.

(pages 5–6)

RESOURCE SHEET 2

From *48 Shades of Brown*:

CHRIS: Oi, Banger!

> DAN *enters, also in uniform and with school bag.*

DAN: Chris.

CHRIS: How was the trip?

DAN: Good. Cold.

CHRIS: Who's this Jack guy? I got a message through the office that Jack had called and I had to sort out your books and timetable and stuff. I thought you were staying with your aunt.

DAN: Yeah, that's Jacq.

> CHRIS *gives him a dubious look.*

Her name's Jacqueline. But no one calls her that.

CHRIS: Jacq. Doesn't sound right for your mother's sister.

DAN: She's not like my mother. She's 23, she's at uni, she plays bass in a band.

CHRIS: And you're staying with this person?

DAN: I'm sharing a house with her, yeah. And another uni student, Naomi.

CHRIS: How old's she?

DAN: 18.

CHRIS: This is sounding good. What's she like?

DAN: She's nice. You'd like Naomi. They're both pretty cool.

CHRIS: Yeah?

DAN: What happened at your place yesterday? Washing? Lawn mowing?

CHRIS: And a barbecue in the afternoon. The cousins came over.

DAN: At my place no one barbecued anything. They drank beer most of the afternoon and Naomi and her boyfriend had sex while I was unpacking my socks.

CHRIS: In your room? With you right there?

   Pause.

DAN: No, in the next room. But the walls are very thin.

(pages 7–8)

RESOURCE SHEET 3

From *48 Shades of Brown*:

CHRIS: Hey, Banger. Where you been?

   DAN *tucks the book under his arm.*

DAN: Library.

CHRIS: So have you got a plan yet?

DAN: Plan?

CHRIS: With Naomi.

DAN: I thought you were going to ease up on the Naomi thing.

CHRIS: Come on, Banger. You've got to at least have a plan. What if she dumps her boyfriend tomorrow and you don't have a plan?

DAN: Give it a rest will, you?

CHRIS: What are you studying? [*He grabs the book.*] *What Bird Is That?*

DAN: On the weekend we were down by the uni lakes and Naomi was very impressed that the scientific names were written on the trees. She said people who know that kind of stuff are very impressive.

CHRIS: And you thought learning tree names was a bit obvious, so you're doing birds.

DAN: Yes.

CHRIS: Ah-ha! I knew you'd have a plan.

DAN: It's more of a strategy, really.

CHRIS: Strategy's good. How does it work?

DAN: I'm not actually going to let her know that I've got an interest at any stage. I'm never going to mention school.

CHRIS: That's good.

DAN: And I'm going to make myself much more interesting.

CHRIS: How would you do that?

DAN: With the bird stuff.

CHRIS: And that's it?

DAN: Yeah. We can be sitting on the veranda or at the uni lakes and I can say, Isn't that a striated thornbill or *Acanthiza Lineata*?

CHRIS: And she'll say, Oh Dan, you've made me into a big sweatball?

DAN: She'll just be impressed.

CHRIS: And you're going to learn all these? There's a lot of birds.

DAN: Just a few basic species and colour types. I mean she's not going to know one duck from another, is she?

CHRIS: *Anas Gibberifrons*, you're going to memorise useless stuff like that?

DAN: What else has twelve years of school equipped me for, Chris, I'm playing to my strengths.

CHRIS: [*skeptical*] I don't know.

DAN: Just a few species and some different shades of brown.

CHRIS: Brown?

DAN: See your average bird, basically, is brown. But not to the expert. We know the difference between say, bright rufous and golden buff, or olive brown and rich chestnut. Or any of the possible 48 shades of brown that I've listed from this book.

CHRIS: Dan.

DAN: What?

CHRIS: Have you thought about getting her drunk?

DAN: This is much more subtle.

CHRIS: But will it work?

DAN: I don't know, Chris. I don't know.

(pages 25–26)

RESOURCE SHEET 4
From *48 Shades of Brown*:

CHRIS: Great party.

DAN: Yeah.

CHRIS: Sorry about the bed. I can't believe I threw up that much.

DAN: Someone else threw up.

CHRIS: I'm pretty sure it was me.

DAN: Someone else, as well as you.

CHRIS: You?

DAN: No, a girl called Imogen.

CHRIS: I had a girl in here? I don't remember. Imogen. Dark hair. Yeah. And I got her into bed? Did I... you know?

DAN: Well, something made her throw up.

CHRIS: Wow.

DAN: You can borrow some clothes if you want. What about your clothes, do you want a garbage bag?

CHRIS: I'll roll it all up in the sleeping bag. What's my mother going to say?

DAN: If only you knew how to use the washing machine.

CHRIS: Life is so complicated.

DAN: Oh, yeah.

(pages 51–52)

www.ingramcontent.com/pod-product-compliance
Lightning Source LLC
Chambersburg PA
CBHW041932090426
42744CB00017B/2026